Weight Watchers Instant Pot Cookbook 2021
200+ Quick & Freestyle WW Instant Pot SmartPoints Recipes for Instant Pot Pressure Cooker

Kathryn Mullins

© Copyright 2021 - All rights reserved

This document is geared towards providing exact and reliable information with regards to the topic and issue covered. The publication is sold with the idea that the publisher is not required to render accounting, officially permitted, or otherwise, qualified services. If advice is necessary, legal, or professional, a practiced individual in the profession should be ordered. - From a Declaration of Principles which was accepted and approved equally by a Committee of the American Bar Association and a Committee of Publishers and Associations. In no way is it legal to reproduce, duplicate, or transmit any part of this document in either electronic means or in printed format. Recording of this publication is strictly prohibited and any storage of this document is not allowed unless with written permission from the publisher.

All rights reserved. The information provided herein is stated to be truthful and consistent, in that any liability, in terms of inattention or otherwise, by any usage or abuse of any policies, processes, or directions contained within is the solitary and utter responsibility of the recipient reader.

Under no circumstances will any legal responsibility or blame be held against the publisher for any reparation, damages, or monetary loss due to the information herein, either directly or indirectly. Respective authors own all copyrights not held by the publisher.

The information herein is offered for informational purposes solely, and is universal as

so. The presentation of the information is without contract or any type of guarantee assurance. The trademarks that are used are without any consent, and the publication of the trademark is without permission or backing by the trademark owner.

All trademarks and brands within this book are for clarifying purposes only and are the owned by the owners themselves, not affiliated with this document.

TABLE OF CONTENTS

Introduction 7

Chapter 1: Everything About the Weight Watchers Freestyle Program 8

Chapter 2: Everything About Weight Watchers Freestyle SmartPoints 15

Chapter 3: Top Tips on Sticking with the Weight Watchers Freestyle Program 17

Chapter 4: Why Use an Instant Pot During Freestyle Program? 19

Chapter 5: Easy and Delicious Weight Watchers Instant Pot Recipes with SmartPoints 26

Pork, Beef and Lamb Recipes 26

1. Spicy Pork Shoulder with Sesame Pickled Cucumbers 26
2. Gratifying Pork Tenderloin with Soy Singer Sauce 27
3. Oozing Apple Butter Pork Chops 27
4. Five-Star Biryani with Lamb 27
5. Astonishing Middle-Eastern Lamb Stew 28
6. Grand Leg of Lamb 29
7. Super Yummy Mediterranean Lamb Roast with Potatoes 29
8. Full-Flavored Lamb and Winter Squash Tagine with Apricots 30
9. Good Tasting Pork Carnitas (Mexican Pulled Pork) 30
10. Magnificent Beef and Broccoli 31
11. Remarkable Cajun Chili 31
12. Phenomenal Chipotle Chili 32
13. Homemade Hamburger Helper 32
14. Famous Spaghetti 33
15. Tempting Beef Short Ribs 33

Chicken, Turkey and Duck Recipes 35

1. Charming Chicken Adobo 35
2. Creamy Garlic Tuscan Chicken Thighs 35
3. Desirable White Chicken Chili 36
4. Rich Honey Teriyaki Chicken 36
5. Enchanting Chicken Cacciatore 36
6. One of a Kind Chicken and Quinoa 37
7. Out Of This World Balsamic Chicken with Tomatoes and Greens 37
8. Summer Italian Chicken 38
9. Delectable Chicken Enchiladas 38

10. Finger Licking Chicken Marsala 39
11. Award Winning Turkey Chili 39
12. Tantalizing Beer-And-Mustard Pulled Turkey 40
13. Extraordinary Honey Garlic Chicken .. 41
14. Refreshing Duck Confit 41
15. Exquisite Orange Duck and Gravy 41

Fish and Seafood Recipes 43
1. Well-Done Seafood Gumbo 43
2. Louisiana-Style Seafood Chicken, and Sausage Gumbo 43
3. Thai Coconut Clams 44
4. Classy Coconut Curry Sea Bass 44
5. Enjoyable Shrimp Paella 45
6. Generous Salmon with Chili-Lime Sauce 45
7. Finger Licking Coconut Fish Curry 46
8. Gorgeous Lemon-Shrimp Risotto with Vegetables and Parmesan 46
9. Nourishing Garlic Butter Salmon and Asparagus 47
10. Pleasant Fish and Potato Chowder 47
11. Soy-Free Asian Salmon 48
12. Traditional Lemon Garlic Salmon 48
13. Decorated Salmon, Broccoli, and Potatoes 49

14. Wonderful in Taste Fish Taco Bowls .. 49
15. Wholesome Clam Chowder 50

Vegan and Vegetarian Recipes 51
1. Legendary Artichokes 51
2. Dazzling Jackfruit Curry 51
3. Deluxe Vegan Barbacoa Mushroom Tacos 51
4. The Number One Vegan Lentil Kidney Bean Chili 52
5. Heavenly Eggplant Sweet Potato Lentil Curry 53
6. Intriguing Vegan Red Lentil, Sweet Potato, Hemp Burgers 53
7. Lip-Smacking Mushroom Stroganoff 54
8. Marvelous Vegan Black Bean Chili 54
9. Indian-Inspired Pickled Potatoes 55
10. Satisfying Vegan Quinoa Burrito Bowls 55
11. Signature Curried Chickpea Stuffed Acorn Squash 56
12. Terrific Vegan Sloppy Joes 56
13. Mexican-Style Corn on the Cob with Hemp-Lime Sauce 57
14. Great Tasting Sweet Potatoes 57
15. To-Die-For Brussel Sprouts with Shallots 57

Rice and Grains Recipes 59
- 1. Incredible Wild Mushroom Rice Risotto 59
- 2. Fantastic Beef Rice Pilaf 59
- 3. Awesome Fried Rice 59
- 4. Welcoming Shrimp Rice 60
- 5. Korean Beef and Brown Rice 60
- 6. Lebanese Hashweh Ground Beef and Rice 61
- 7. Tastiest Mexican Black Beans and Rice 61
- 8. Kheema Pulao (Indian Meat and Rice) 62
- 9. Sensational Chicken and Rice 62
- 10. Scrumptious Mexican Rice 63

Soups, Stews, and Broths Recipes 64
- 1. Worldwide Vegetable Soup 64
- 2. Hearty Vegetable and Brown Rice Soup 64
- 3. Beyond This World Tomato Soup 65
- 4. Creamy Tortellini, Spinach, and Chicken Soup 65
- 5. Overpowering Wild Rice Soup 66
- 6. Spicy Sweet Potato Chili 66
- 7. Lemon Chicken Noodle Soup 67
- 8. Wonderful Buffalo Chicken Chili 67
- 9. Godly Coconut Curry Butternut Squash Soup 67
- 10. Famous French Onion Soup 68
- 11. Amazing Zuppa Toscana 68
- 12. Lovely Curry Cauliflower and Broccoli Soup 69
- 13. Flavorful Chicken Tortilla-Less Soup . 69
- 14. Curried Carrot Red Lentil Soup 70
- 15. Scrumptious Sausage Italian Lentil and Barley Soup 70
- 16. Delectable Curry Pumpkin 71
- 17. Hearty Golden Lentil and Spinach Soup 71
- 18. Delicious Italian Farmhouse Vegetable Soup 72
- 19. Creamy Cauliflower Soup 72
- 20. Supreme Taco Soup 73
- 21. Yummy Tomato Spinach Soup 73
- 22. Flavorsome Chunky Beef, Cabbage, and Tomato Soup 74
- 23. Unique Loaded Baked Potato Soup 74
- 24. Exquisite Broccoli Cheese Soup 75

Appetizers and Side Dishes Recipes 76
- 1. Candied Pecans 76
- 2. Delicious Roasted Onion Garlic Hummus 76

3. Great Tasting Broccoli and Cheddar Pasta 77

4. Creamy Macaroni and Cheese 77

5. Lovely Meatballs 77

6. Party-Perfect Black Bean Dip 78

7. Sweet and Spicy Meatballs 78

8. Enjoyable Pizza Dip 79

9. Artichoke and Spinach Dip 79

10. Appetizing Tomato Mac and Cheese with Crispy Bacon 79

11. Buffalo Hot Wings 80

12. Pleasant Cheddar Bacon Ale Dip 80

13. Cheesy Rotel Queso Dip 81

14. Cabbage with Turkey Sausage 81

15. Fit for a King Spinach Artichoke Macaroni and Cheese 82

16. Smoky Baked Beans 82

17. Classic Potato Salad 83

18. Contest-Winning Chili Con Carne 83

19. Drive-Thru Tacos 84

20. Fun to Eat Monkey Bread 84

21. Perfect Little Smokies 85

Desserts Recipes 86

1. Beautiful Lemon-Blueberry Bundt Cake 86

2. Sensational Apples with Oats 86

3. Best Chocolate Pudding 86

4. Great Lemon Buttermilk Bundt Cake ... 87

5. Secret Chocolate Cupcakes 88

6. Satisfying Blueberry Compote 88

7. Elegant Blackberry Cobbler 88

8. Glorious Chocolate Chip Bundt Cake ... 89

9. Enticing Pumpkin Chocolate Chip Bundt Cake 89

10. Delightful Banana Chocolate-Chip Mini Muffins 90

Chapter 6: 14-Day Healthy Weight Watchers Meal Plan for Beginners 91

The Final Words 93

Cooking and Culinary Units Conversion Chart 94

Introduction

I wish to personally congratulate you and thank you for purchasing, *"Weight Watchers Instant Pot Cookbook 2021: 200+ Quick & Freestyle WW Instant Pot SmartPoints Recipes for Instant Pot Pressure Cooker"*. **This is the only book you will need to lose weight and finally get healthy.**

A large percentage of people around the world are overweight and they struggle to lose weight is real. You have probably heard tons of different advice on the Internet on how to lose weight. Thousands of books on dieting and exercising on the market. But did any of it work? Probably not. Some weight loss methods and diets require too much time or too much effort.

Then there are the diets and weight loss advice that just doesn't work. A lot of the crash diets and instant weight loss secrets can actually be damaging to your body and overall health. So, it's understandable why some people are unsuccessful at losing weight. Luckily for you, this book introduces the easy Weight Watchers diet which will work for anyone who is willing to give it a shot.

The diet includes pasta, steak, fried chicken, cheeseburger, ice cream, cookies, vegetables… yes, you can eat just about anything on Weight Watchers. Weight Watchers works by a point system which is geared to help you make healthier food decisions and encourage physical activity, so you can lose weight permanently. Weight Watchers technically isn't a diet, it's more of a lifestyle-change program.

This Weight Watchers Instant Pot Cookbook will allow you to learn to make some of the most delicious meals on the planet and more. It includes all sorts of recipes and the cooking instructions for preparing those amazing dishes. The Smart Points value and recipe nutrition are also given for every recipe as well. We have done our very best to include a diverse set of recipes to please everyone. Here you will find meals ready to be served for **breakfast, lunches, dinner, and for beans and grains, beef and pork, lamb, chicken, duck, fish and seafood, vegetables, and side dishes, soups and stews, poultry, and desserts**. Just about everything you can think of.

This book also features the amazing Instant Pot which is a genius kitchen gadget. The Instant Pot is a multi-use, 7-in-1 programmable cookers that combine the functions and capabilities of a pressure cooker, slow cooker, rice cooker, cake maker, yogurt maker, steamer, warmer, saute pan, and sterilizer. The Instant Pot works by sealing the lid so that pressure builds up inside the pot. The food is exposed in a pressurized environment which cooks food quicker and retains more vitamins and minerals than other cooking methods.

This book will open a new world of incredibly delicious and healthy foods to you. At the end of the book, you will find a Weight Watchers meal plan, which will give you a great start for your Weight Watchers journey. Use this book daily as it contains tons of healthy and incredibly tasty recipes that will satisfy your stomach and help you lose weight.

Thanks again for reading the book, I hope that you will enjoy it!

Chapter 1: Everything About the Weight Watchers Freestyle Program

Want to lose weight and still enjoy all your favorite foods? Then attempt on the Weight Watchers Freestyle Program. In this chapter, you will learn everything about Weight Watchers and how you can get started.

Key Principles of Successful Weight Watchers Freestyle and How It Works

Weight Watchers is an effective program because it's not really a diet. There are no specific restrictions on food intake, you just pay careful attention to portion sizes and keep track of SmartPoints.

Weight Watchers is less strict than many other diets – but the results are still promising, with participants able to lose up to 2- 4 pounds per week. This program still follows the three key principles: **Keep track of what you eat using SmartPoints, make healthy habits, and join a support group.**

Joining Weight Watchers, you learn how to calculate the number of SmartPoints to achieve your health and weight loss goals. Your daily and weekly SmartPoints allowance will be different depending on each person's status. After you are given a personalized SmartPoint limit, you get to decide which foods to eat based on the SmartPoints value appointed to each meal. No foods are banned on the program, the only rule is not to go over your SmartPoints allowance. *Foods that are nutritious, healthy, and filling tend to have fewer SmartPoints, while high-fat, and high-carb meals tend to have larger SmartPoints value*.

This plan gives you the opportunity to choose healthy foods over the unhealthy ones. Some dieters even combine Weight Watchers with other diets such as the low-carb diet. It also means dieters won't have a hard time adopting this diet. You can follow the plan right this very second and it pretty much won't affect your day to day living.

The objective is to make better health decisions and lose weight in an unintimidating manner. It also heavily encourages including exercise and joining a support group. You are welcome to track your physical activity and exercise through activity trackers such as Fitbit. Here you will look at what exercise you are doing and how it will fit alongside your diet.

The third principle is joining a support group where you can meet like-minded people who share similar goals. You will also have a success coach watching over you who have been on the same journey as you. This is essential for the Weight Watchers program, and statistically, the more you attend the meetings, the higher your chance of weight loss success.

A Brief History of the Weight Watchers Freestyle Program

The history of the Weight Watchers program is easy to follow.

In early 1961, American business entrepreneur and co-founder of the Weight Watchers organization, Jean Nidetch had struggled with weight for most of her life and gone through every crazy diet out there where the weight was always coming back.

She gathered friends and members to her apartment every week to discuss their tips, achievements, and journey on losing weight. She later established a point system for foods to keep track of. This way dieters can focus eating more lean protein, fruits and vegetables and less sugar and saturated fat to lose weight.

By the end of 1962, Jean had lost more than 32 kilograms and many other participants shared similar results undergoing this program.

In 1962, the company Weight Watchers was founded and has grown immensely. The Weight Watchers program has attracted many celebrities such as Oprah Winfrey, Jessica, Simpson and Mariah Carey.

To this day, the Weight Watchers program has helped millions of people around the globe achieve their weight loss goals.

Ins and Outs of the Weight Watchers Diet

Weight Watchers is a widely popular and successful weight-loss program that has helped millions of people around the globe. But that doesn't necessarily mean it's right for everyone. It's essential you take a look at all the advantages and disadvantages of the Weight Watchers program before you commit.

Ins of Weight Watchers Freestyle

Here are some reasons why the diet plan may be the best route to help you lose weight.

- **No restrictions on food:** There is no official list of foods to avoid on Weight Watchers like you'll see on other diets. Instead, you track SmartPoints and garner FitPoints. The point system encourages you to eat more healthy foods such as fruits and vegetables while also enjoying your favorite sweets occasionally.
- **Nutritional value tips, cooking advice, recipes, and lifestyle changes are offered:** When you attend Weight Watchers meetings, meeting leaders is inclined to share effective nutritional advice with participants, for example, discussing the importance of adding more vegetables, healthy fats, low-fat dairy, reduced sugar, and drinking plenty of water to your diet.
- **The program is eligible for kids:** Some Weight Watchers locations hold meetings open for children. Teens as young as 13-years-old can participate in the Weight Watchers program if they have physician approval.
- **Slow and steady weight loss:** If you choose to commit to this program, you can expect to lose 1 to 2 pounds per week. You might lose even more when you first begin. Losing weight at a slow and steady rate makes weight loss more stable.
- **The program encourages portion control:** In order to keep track and record your SmartPoints you will need to measure your portions and serving sizes. Being able to control your portions will benefit you beyond Weight Watchers.
- **The program encourages exercise:** The Weight Watchers program encourages daily exercise which earns you FitPoints. Earning FitPoints will balance out your food intake.
- **You will cook at home:** You are more likely to eat healthy foods if you prepare them yourself at home. Weight Watchers offers recipes using your Instant Pot to help you learn how to prepare healthy meals.

Outs of Weight Watchers Freestyle

While Weight Watchers is a perfect solution for many to lose weight, it may not be appropriate for you. Take a look at the disadvantages of the Weight Watchers program.

- **Weight Watchers can be pricey:** The monthly cost for joining the Weight Watchers program will vary based on the level you choose, but if you have a substantial amount of weight to lose, the investment may be costly.
- **Group meetings aren't for everyone:** Some people prefer to keep their personal health and weight loss information private. You are not required to talk at Weight Watchers meetings. But Weight Watchers meetings are what makes the program special. However, if you prefer to avoid meetings, there are other options.
- **Weekly weigh-ins are a must:** Weighing yourself once a week to track your progress on the Weight Watchers program is a requirement. For some participants, this can be uncomfortable. For others, it keeps them motivated.
- **Weekly progress may discourage you:** Weekly progress checks can vary. Some weeks you will lose little weight. Sometimes you may even gain weight, even if you're doing everything right. This can discourage you from remaining in the program.
- **Keeping track of SmartPoints:** Keeping track of all the SmartPoints can be tedious and time-consuming.
- **Freedom to eat:** The Weight Watchers diet don't have any restrictions and you can eat almost anything you want. This freedom to eat anything you want can be too tempting. For some participants, diets that offer strict eating guidelines prove more effective.

Weight Watchers Freestyle: Foods You Can Eat

One reason why Weight Watchers Program is so popular is that there is no official restriction on what you can eat. The main objective of Weight Watchers is to keep track of your SmartPoints which helps control what you eat to lose weight.

Zero-point foods are foods that are low in saturated fat, sugar, carb, and calorie content. You should eat zero points foods as much as you can to help you lose weight, control your hunger, and stick with the Weight Watchers program. Here is the complete list of zero points foods which can help you make healthier food choices.

- Apples
- Unsweetened applesauce
- Apricots
- Arrowroots
- Artichoke hearts
- Artichokes
- Arugula
- Asparagus
- Bamboo shoots
- Banana
- Adzuki beans
- Black beans
- Green beans
- Chickpeas
- Great Northern beans
- Kidney beans
- Lima beans
- White beans
- Soybeans
- Navy beans
- Beets
- Berries
- Blackberries
- Blueberries
- Broccoli
- Brussel sprouts
- Green cabbage
- Red cabbage
- Bok choy
- Calamari
- Cantaloupe
- Carrots
- Cauliflower
- Caviar
- Celery
- Swiss chard
- Cherries
- Ground chicken breast
- Chicken breast or tenderloin
- Coleslaw mix
- Collards
- Corn
- White corn

- Cranberries
- Cucumber
- Daikon
- Dates
- Dragon fruit
- Egg substitutes
- Egg whites
- Eggplant
- Whole eggs
- Endive
- Fennel
- Figs
- Anchovies
- Sea Bass
- Carp
- Catfish
- Butterfish
- Cod
- Eel
- Haddock
- Halibut
- Herring
- Mackerel
- Monkfish
- Rainbow trout
- Rockfish
- Roe
- Salmon
- Sardines
- Seabass
- Striped mullet
- Swordfish
- Tuna
- Whitefish
- Tilapia
- Fruit cocktail
- Unsweetened fruit cup
- Fruit salad
- Unsweetened fruit
- Garlic
- Ginger root
- Grapefruit
- Grapes
- Honeydew melon
- Jackfruit

- Jerk chicken breast
- Kiwifruit
- Leeks
- Lemon
- Lemon zest
- Lentils
- Lettuce
- Lime
- Lime zest
- Mangoes
- Melon
- Brown mushrooms
- Button mushrooms
- Cremini mushrooms
- Italian mushrooms
- Portabella mushrooms
- Shiitake mushrooms
- Okra
- Onions
- Oranges
- Blood oranges
- Papayas
- Parsley
- Passionfruit
- Pears
- Peaches
- Peas
- Black-eyed peas
- Split peas
- Cayenne peppers
- Jalapeno peppers
- Poblano peppers
- Sweet bell peppers
- Pepperoncini
- Unsweetened pickles
- Pineapple
- Plumcots
- Plums
- Pomegranate seeds
- Pomegranate
- Pumpkin
- Pumpkin puree
- Radishes
- Radishes
- Raspberries

- Salsa verde
- Fat-free salsa
- Sauerkraut
- Scallions
- Seaweed
- Scallions
- Shallots
- Clams
- Crabs
- Crabmeat
- Crayfish
- Lobster
- Mussels
- Octopus
- Oysters
- Scallops
- Shrimp
- Squid
- Spinach
- Sprouts
- Summer squash
- Winter squash
- Zucchini
- Strawberries
- Tofu
- Tomatoes
- Tomato puree
- Tomato sauce
- Turkey
- Turnips
- Vegetable stick
- Mixed vegetables
- Water chestnuts
- Watermelon
- Greek yogurt
- Plain yogurt
- Soy yogurt

A Word of Caution on Zero Point Foods

Zero-point foods are the best thing about the Weight Watchers program but this may lead to slower weight loss. You should try to eat zero-point foods in moderation and only when you're hungry.

Do your best not to overeat and control your portion sizes even if it is zero-point foods. For example, while eggs are zero points, it isn't recommended to have an 8-egg omelet for breakfast.

Weight Watchers Freestyle: Foods to Avoid

In the Weight Watchers, you should avoid foods with high SmartPoints value. ***Food that are high in refined carbs and fats and low protein tend to have a higher point value in the Weight Watchers program.***

Such food items include cupcakes, cookies, ice cream, cheeseburgers, pasta, chili cheese fries, deep fried chicken, and cherry pies. Most foods served at fast food restaurants tend to have over 20 points! A triple whopper with cheese is 31 points!

So, what foods should you think twice on? Fast foods, junk foods, and sugary drinks are the absolute worst to eat if you want to feel satiated while cutting your caloric intake. This also includes many foods made with flour, gluten, or added sugar and most high-fat foods. These foods taste luxuriant but are loaded with fat and calories. Because of this, we eat them so fast that we eat too much before we feel satiated.

This doesn't mean you must cut all your favorite treats out of your diet entirely. Remember, you can eat anything on the Weight Watchers program, but only in moderation. Don't think you can eat a Bacon Cheeseburger Deluxe for lunch every day and expect to lose 2 pounds a week.

Chapter 2: Everything About Weight Watchers Freestyle SmartPoints

The Weight Watchers program is based on a SmartPoint system which tracks the food you eat. This system encourages dieters to choose highly nutritious and healthy foods rather than junk food. In this chapter, you will learn everything you need to know about Weight Watchers Freestyle SmartPoints.

What are SmartPoints and How Does It Work?

SmartPoints is a revitalization of the counting ProPoint system that is quite easy to understand.

SmartPoints encourages you to make nutritious, healthier informed food decisions so that you choose food that make you feel better, have more energy and lose weight as opposed to unhealthy food. Hence, the reason why they are called SmartPoints.

With SmartPoints, foods that are greater in sugar and saturated fat have higher SmartPoints values. Foods with more lean protein lower the SmartPoints value. This directs you towards healthier food decisions.

Every food, every meal, every recipe has their own SmartPoints value that is based on calories, sugar, protein, and saturated fat. The more protein decreases the SmartPoints value while saturated fat and sugar increase the SmartPoints value.

How does it work?

When you join the Weight Watchers program, you will be given a customized SmartPoints budget which is influenced by your current weight, height, gender, and age.

SmartPoints also have a daily allowance, in addition to a weekly allowance to use on splurges, cravings, or larger portions. It's also easy to keep track of your SmartPoints value which in return allow you to make healthier and more gratifying food decisions.

Healthy eating habits that work best for you.

Counting SmartPoints you can eat anything you like – nothing is off limits. You will be losing weight by eating tasty foods that fill you up. Using this system gives you the freedom and flexibility to enjoy your food preferences and lose weight.

Example Calculation of SmartPoints

We want to help you calculate Weight Watchers SmartPoints so you can enjoy all sorts of food. In this section, you will learn how to calculate SmartPoints for your favorite dishes.

Before you begin the program, you will need to be aware of one small adjustment to the SmartPoints system. Weight Watchers is now focusing on other contents such as saturated fats and sugars. So, while a honeybun used to be 2 points, it will now be 6 points. This promotes more awareness of your food choices.

The new Weight Watchers program has a daily limit of 30 points rather than 26. So, this change makes you rethink reaching for a bowl of ice cream instead of fresh fruit.

How to Calculate Weight Watchers SmartPoints

The math behind Weight Watchers points is complicated to calculate unless you are a licensed nutritionist. I recommend you use an online Weight Watchers SmartPoints calculator.

Using an online calculator, you will need to provide the calories, saturated fats, sugar, and protein content that is found on the recipe nutrition label.

Site: http://www.calculatorcat.com/health/weight-watchers-calculator.html

How to Calculate Recipe Calories and Nutrition

Some nutrition analyzers you find online don't provide the proper information you in. The best in-depth calorie and nutrition calculator is VeryWellFit.com recipe analyzer.

You can enter practically any ingredient into the recipe analyzer and it gives you the full nutrition information for the whole recipe. Take note of calories, fats, sugar, and protein content

Take note of calories, fats, sugar, and protein per recipe and enter those numbers into the Calculator Cat tool above to figure out the total SmartPoints per recipe.

Divide that number by servings and you will have the SmartPoints value for literally any recipe you have.

Site: https://www.verywellfit.com/recipe-nutrition-analyzer-4157076

The two tools mentioned above will be a useful and effective tool to have in order to calculate recipes and nutrition information for your favorite foods and meals.

Remember to choose healthy foods with low Weight Watchers SmartPoints to find any success in this program.

Your Weight Loss Expectations

Healthy and permanent weight loss is achieved gradually, at a rate of no quicker than 2 pounds per week. The program follows this rule, where dieters can expect to lose 1 to 2 pounds per week on average. But, several factors can change this number. It is advisable to consult your physician or doctor before starting Weight Watchers.

Measuring weight loss

Fat loss main principle is to burn more calories than you consume to achieve weight loss. However, weight loss is much more complicated.

Weight is the force of gravity measured on a weighing scale. For example, weight yourself before and after a large meal and a few cups of water. You'll notice significant differences. For the most precise weight loss log, the Handbook of Obesity Treatment suggests it's best to weigh yourself at the same time of the day once per week without any clothes.

Factors in first-week weight loss

Many people lose more weight their first week on the Weight Watchers program than the weeks after. This is primarily because of weight loss, caused by decreasing sodium intake and increasing your water intake.

Weight Watchers

Weight watchers cause weight loss by helping you reduce your calorie intake.

There are no restrictions on the Weight Watchers program. Instead, all foods are allowed but only in moderation.

The plan is designed to give an incentive to opt for low-fat, high fiber foods rather than high-fat, low-fiber foods. These foods are unprocessed and low in sodium. With this said, Weight Watchers dieters can expect to lose up to 2 pounds to 4 pounds during their first week following the program.

The Weight Watchers program was created to educate you on portion control to gradually lose weight and maintain a healthy body weight.

Don't freak out about how much weight you lost during any week, including your first week on the program. It can be tempting to give up if your first week didn't meet your expectations. Focus on making healthy food decisions and remember that permanent weight loss is a lifestyle change.

Chapter 3: Top Tips on Sticking with the Weight Watchers Freestyle Program

There are several useful strategies and advice that will help you get started on the Weight Watchers program. Below are top tips that will help you succeed in Weight Watchers:

Drink lots of water: Drinking water is essential for health, and it's going to help immeasurably in the Weight Watchers program. Drinking water also has many benefits including easier weight loss, clear skin, improved digestion, more energy, and increased mental clarity.

Learn portion control: Learning portion control is extremely important in Weight Watchers. You must be able to recognize ounces and cups when dining out or even cooking at home. If you can control portion and serving sizes, this can help ease the path to successful weight loss.

Don't overeat fruit: Fruits are zero SmartPoints food value because it is encouraged for dieters to eat them. They make good snacks and highly nutritious. So, don't be afraid to eat them. However, only eat fruit until you're satisfied, not full. It is recommended to eat only five servings of fruit per day.

Figure out your why: Motivation is crucial for weight loss. You will be more motivated to lose weight after you know why you want to lose weight in the first place. Some reasons include: having more energy, lowering your cholesterol, live longer, or look better. Find out why you committed to Weight Watchers program and remind yourself of it every day.

Don't guess SmartPoints: The most important thing to understand about SmartPoints is that you cannot guess SmartPoint values. The calculation of SmartPoints goes beyond calories. The calorie count you find on nutrition labels is based on the amount of energy in a food before it enters your body. After you consume it, your body processes it. As it processes the food, a portion of the food's calories is burned for body energy. SmartPoints are calculated based on the energy that is available after your body processed a food. This means you cannot just look at a food label and guess how much SmartPoints there is. You will over guess and throw the entire point system off balance.

Eat as many zero Points foods as you can: Take a look at the zero Points food list by Weight Watchers. There is plenty of tasty foods you can eat from and it's highly recommended to choose foods with zero points value whenever you can.

Don't cheat: If you want to eat something that is 9 points, and you only have 8 points left for the day, don't eat it believing it won't hurt you. It will really affect your body, diet, and mentality by adding that extra point. To find success in this program, you must be honest with yourself.

Share your journey: When you tell someone about your journey and progress, you are more likely to stay on track. You can participate in Weight Watchers meetings where you share your experience with other participants and leaders. You can even talk with someone, not on the diet, just someone who is supportive and makes you the most comfortable.

Plan your meals: By planning your meals ahead of time, it will help keep track of your SmartPoints throughout the day. If you're planning on dining out, figure out what you're going to order before you leave. If you're not a fan of meal prep, maybe you should start getting into the habit of it.

Track everything: Track your SmartPoints as you go. It's recommended that you carry a small notebook or have a tracking app on your phone. If you wait till before you sleep, you will probably forget some meals and snacks you had earlier today.

Don't forget exercise: Find ways to become more active and to move more in your life. When people lose weight through dieting, they tend to think that exercise is no longer necessary. They're wrong. You can lose weight quicker and become more fit if you include regular aerobic and cardio exercise in your life.

Expect progress, not perfection: Don't set yourself up for failure by seeking perfection. Don't set impossible goals. As you start the Weight Watchers program, you will go through days where you feel unmotivated and see no progress and you will go through days where you feel like you're on top of the world.

Be patient with yourself: While other diets may be too strict or just not working, the Weight Watchers program does work but it takes time to notice significant results. Remember, the Weight

Watchers program is more of a lifestyle change than a diet. You won't find overnight success joining this program. You must be patient with yourself and not fight the change.

Eat high water content fruits and vegetables: If you can't drink a big jug of water, try eating high water content fruits and vegetables instead. Below you will find a list of high water content fruit and veggies.

Fruit and water content:
- Watermelon, 92% water content
- Strawberry, 92% water content
- Grapefruit, 91% water content
- Cantaloupe, 90% water content
- Peach, 88% water content
- Pineapple, 87% water content
- Cranberry, 87% water content
- Orange, 87% water content
- Raspberry, 87% water content
- Apricot, 86% water content
- Blueberry, 85% water content
- Plum, 85% water content
- Apple, 84% water content
- Pear, 84% water content
- Cherry, 81% water content
- Grape, 81% water content
- Banana, 74% water content

Veggies and water content:
- Cucumber, 96% water content
- Lettuce, 96% water content
- Zucchini, 95% water content
- Radish, 95% water content
- Celery, 95% water content
- Tomato, 94% water content
- Green cabbage, 93% water content
- Cauliflower, 92% water content
- Eggplant, 92% water content
- Red cabbage, 92% water content
- Pepper, 92% water content
- Spinach, 92% water content
- Broccoli, 91% water content
- Carrots, 87% water content
- Green pea, 79% water content
- Potato, 79% water content

Keep a Weight Watchers diary: Studies show that Weight Watchers participants who don't keep a food diary have a tougher time losing weight. It is recommended that you keep daily food records to successfully follow the Weight Watchers program and maintain steady weight loss.

I want you to find success with your health and your weight loss journey. In order to achieve this, you must follow the Weight Watchers program, but learn how to modify your entire way of thinking. The tips above will help you find ultimate success in your physical, mental, and financial health journey.

If you want to learn more dieting tips, look at WeightWatchers.com community message boards.

Chapter 4: Why Use an Instant Pot During Freestyle Program?

So, why should you include an Instant Pot in the weight watchers program?

The Instant Pot is an electric pressure cooker that combines 7 kitchen appliances in 1 pressure cooker, which includes:

1. Pressure Cooker
2. Slow Cooker
3. Rice/Congee/Porridge Maker
4. Steamer
5. Sauté/browning
6. Yogurt Maker
7. Warmer/Cancel

It can make nutritious and healthy meals in an effective manner. In this chapter, you will learn all about the Instant Pot and how to get the most from it.

Overview of the Instant Pot

The Instant Pot is a revolutionary modern electric pressure cooker that is sweeping the nation.

There are many types of electric pressure cookers on the market, but the Instant Pot is truly unique due to its remarkable features. The Instant Pot plenty of additional features which makes it different from other types of electric pressure cookers.

For example, unlike other types of electric pressure cookers, the Instant Pot has a "Sauté" feature where you can sauté/brown your foods right in your Instant Pot by a push of a button with the lid removed. This can serve especially useful when starting soups, stews, and even making yogurt.

The Instant Pot also has a feature for keeping your food warm for up to 10 hours once a dish is done the cooking.

Not only does the Instant Pot comes with lots of additional features, but it's also safer and more convenient than a standard stovetop pressure cooker. The Instant Pot was designed with 10 safety mechanisms which ensure that the pot doesn't over pressurized.

All you need to do is dump all the food ingredients in the pot, lock the lid, press a few buttons, and allowing the Instant Pot to work its magic.

All About the Buttons on Your Instant Pot

So, you're ready to start cooking with your brand new Instant Pot Electric Pressure Cooker but you don't know what all those 'weird' Instant Pot buttons do.

Don't sweat it, in this section, you will learn all about the buttons on your Instant Pot. Take a look in this section if you're ever confused on the functions in the future.

Sauté: Press the Sauté function to sauté vegetables, brown meats, and simmer ingredients in the pressure cooking pot with the lid removed. The "Adjust" button can be used to set the cooking pot to one of these three temperature ranges: "normal" (320 to 349 degrees Fahrenheit), "more" (347 to 410 degrees Fahrenheit), and "less" (275 to 302 degrees Fahrenheit).

Manual: Most recipes in this cookbook ask you to cook at High Pressure, this is the button you press. Once you press it, you can adjust the cooking time using the [+] and [-] buttons. When the Instant Pot beeps it will start the pressure cooking process.

Keep Warm/Cancel: Press this button to cancel any button or to turn off your Instant Pot. Your Instant Pot will automatically enter this mode at the end of your selected cooking program.

[-] and [+] Button: Press this button to adjust the cooking time.

Less | Normal | More: This button can be used to adjust the cooking temperature by repeatedly pressing the button until you reach the desired setting.

Soup/Broth: This button will automatically cook at High Pressure for 30 minutes.

Meat/Stew: This button will automatically cook at High Pressure for 35 minutes.

Bean/Chili: This button will automatically cook at High Pressure for 30 minutes.

Poultry: This button will automatically cook at High Pressure for 15 minutes.

Rice: This button will automatically cook at Low Pressure and the cooking time will depend on the amount of water and rice in the cooking pot.

Multigrain: This button will automatically cook at High Pressure for 30 minutes.

Porridge/Congee: This button will cook at High Pressure for 20 minutes.

Steam: This button will automatically cook at High Pressure for 10 minutes. Use this button with a trivet or steamer back inside your pressure cooker.

Slow Cook: This button will automatically slow cook for 4 hours. Press the [+] and [-] to adjust the cooking time.

Yogurt: This function is used to making yogurt.

Cake: This button will cook at High Pressure for 40 minutes. (This button can only be found on newer Instant Pot models)

Egg: This button will cook at High Pressure for 4 minutes. (This button can only be found with newer Instant Pot models)

Sterilize: This button can be used to sterilize cooking utensils and pasteurizing milk for yogurt-making. (This button can only be found on newer models)

Pressure/Pressure Level Button: This button can switch the pressure cooking between High Pressure and Low Pressure.

Timer Button/Delay Start: This button can set the timer to delay cooking for up to 24 hours.

The Two Methods of Releasing Pressure from Your Instant Pot

As pressure builds up inside your Instant Pot it will need to be released before you can remove the lid. The pressure inside the Instant Pot pressure cooker can be released in two different ways. The two methods include:

The Natural Release Method: This method allows the pressure to naturally release by itself. This method takes approximately about 10 to 30 minutes to depressurize naturally depending on the volume of liquid in the cooking pot. The more liquid content, the longer it takes to depressurize.

The Quick Release Method: To quick release the pressure, all you need to do is turn the valve from "sealing" to "venting". This releases the pressure from your pot as fast as it can, depressurization only takes 1 minute or so.

Some recipes require you to natural release the pressure before you perform the quick release method. For this, you will want to either unplug the Instant Pot or press the Keep Warm/Cancel button, and wait the number of minutes listed in the instructions. Then, turn the valve to release the remaining pressure that is built up in the pressure cooker. This allows the food to cook longer in a slower cooking environment.

How to Use the Instant Pot?

If you're new to the Instant Pot, you should know it's easy to use.

Before you begin cooking with your Instant Pot, it's important that you read the user manual to learn about the parts and what it does. Also, take the "Instant Pot Water Test" before preparing any real recipes using the Instant Pot. Here's how:

1. Pour 2 cups of cold water to the inner pot in the Instant Pot.
2. Close the Instant Pot lid, and lock the lid by turning clockwise direction.
3. Press the Manual button and adjust the time to 2 minutes.
4. When the timer beeps, either quick release or naturally release the pressure.

Congratulations! You've passed the test!

The water test will demonstrate how the pressure works. Once you're finished with that, ensure you read the recipe all the way through before you start cooking.

How to Saute/Brown Food in your Instant Pot

The saute function is used to do the following:

- Saute: Many recipes ask for you to saute onions/garlic/aromatics, you can cook them directly using the low saute mode.
- Reduce sauces/liquid: If you need to reduce liquid in your Instant Pot, press the saute function and continue to cook until you reach the desired consistency.
- Sear meats: Press the saute button and add a bit of oil. Once the oil is hot, add the meat and sear for 4 to 5 minutes or until brown.
- Bringing the Instant Pot to pressure faster: Your Instant Pot will take a few minutes to build up the pressure until the timer begins to pressure cook. You can speed up the pressure building process by pressing the saute button to heat ingredients. Once hot, press Keep Warm/Cancel button, and press the manual button and adjust the cooking time.

Best Things to Cook in Your Instant Pot

Anything you can make in a slow cooker can be made in the Instant Pot, but just faster. Here are other things you can make in your Instant Pot:

- Soups can be made in your Instant Pot which usually takes 5 to 10 minutes.
- Stews typically take 35 minutes of cooking time.
- Dried beans, if you forgot to soak beans, you can presoak them in your Instant Pot.
- All vegetables
- Rice
- Risotto
- Oatmeal
- Caramelized onions
- Whole chicken roast
- Sauces
- Meatballs in sauce
- Reheating meals
- And much more!

Why should I use my Instant Pot instead of the stovetop/oven?

The Instant Pot comes with tons of benefits, including:
- The Instant Pot doesn't use much energy which can save you some money on your electrical bill.
- The Instant Pot is safer to use than most pressure cookers.
- Food cooked in your Instant Pot tastes better because pressure cooing uses a high temperature which brings out more flavor from your foods.
- The Instant Pot cook foods faster than most cooking methods today. This makes it especially popular for chefs to use in restaurants.
- The food is much healthier because vitamins and minerals cannot escape from the food as its cooked in an airtight container.

<u>Helpful Instant Pot Tips and Tricks You Need to Know</u>

Learn about the best Instant Pot tips and tricks to make your experience much easier.
- Always have ½ to 1 cup of chicken broth or water in the pot when cooking. The liquid is needed in the inner pot to build up steam to cook foods. This is an incredibly important rule to remember when you use your Instant Pot for pressure cooking. Pressure cooking in your Instant Pot without any liquid can either undercook or overcook your meals.
- Your Instant Pot is not so different as a cooking skillet or frying pan. You can practically cook anything you usually make using a skillet or frying pan in your Instant Pot by pressing the saute function. The saute function doesn't require any water but it does need some oil or butter. You can adjust the saute temperature as needed.
- Don't forget to seal the lid: If you're in a hurry, it can be easy to forget to seal the lid. If you do forget to seal the lid, the Instant Pot will not be able to pressure cook.

- Don't overfill your Instant Pot. Only fill your Instant Pot up to the fill line and allow enough room to take in expanding rice, beans, legumes, and grains.
- Don't open the Instant Pot while in Manual/Pressure mode. Once you lock the lid and press Manual/Pressure mode, make sure you don't open the lid. This will ensure proper pressure cooking. If you remove the lid, the pressure will quickly escape and need to start the entire pressure building process all over again. So, once you lock the lid, allow it to cook until the timer beeps before removing the lid.
- Don't quick release pressure if you are cooking soups, stews, or foods with large liquid volume. Choose natural release instead.
- Have two sets of inner pots and lids. This way you can cook food in one pot and use the other pot to prepare another dish.

Top Instant Pot Mistakes to Avoid

There's a handful of mistakes you can make as a new owner of the Instant Pot. Here are some common mistakes to avoid as a new Instant Pot user so you can be successful at using your Instant Pot.

- Don't overfill your Instant Pot. Every Instant Pot has a max fill line in the inner pot. If you fill liquid over this fill line you could risk jamming the venting knob. In the case of filling over the max fill line, use natural pressure release to alleviate the pressure and discard the extra liquid.
- Don't quick release if you are cooking soups or food with high liquid volume. If you quick release the pressure when making foamy foods, you risk a hot splattering mess.
- You press the timer button instead of cooking time. It's easy to mistake the timer button with the cooking button.
- You press the timer button when setting the cooking time. It's easy to mistake those two buttons. The timer button is used to delay cooking, while the cooking time is used to how long your food will cook for.
- Not using heat resistant towels or oven mitts. The Instant Pot lid can be very hot and you could risk harming yourself removing the lid without using an oven mitt or towel when venting.
- You put your Instant Pot on the stove. Some users mistakenly put their Instant Pot on the stove which can increase the risk of burning the bottom of the Instant Pot.
- Some users make the mistake of using the rice button on just any type of rice or grain. The rice setting is used to make white rice. Different types of rice (such as brown rice) require different volumes of water to rice ratios, and this will affect the cooking time.
- Using hot liquid instead of cold liquid. If you use hot liquid instead of cold liquid, this can lead to undercooking your meals and reducing the cooking time.

Instant Pot Cooking Time for Various Foods

Many factors can affect the cooking time for various foods. For example, cooking temperature, type of meat, and thickness of the meat may require more or less cooking time to reach a certain level of tenderness or textures.

When cooking frozen food in a pressure cooker, you don't need to microwave the food to defrost. However, frozen food might call for a longer preheating and cook time depending on the amount of food inside your pressure cooker.

Below you will find the general cooking times for the listed various foods:
- Beans, legumes, and lentils
- Meat (poultry, beef, pork, and lamb)
- Seafood and fish
- Rice and grains
- Vegetables
- Fruits

Seafood and Fish – Cooking Time Guidelines

- Fresh whole crab, 2 to 3 minutes
- Frozen whole crab, 4 to 5 minutes

- Fresh whole fish, 4 to 5 minutes
- Frozen whole fish, 5 to 7 minutes
- Fresh fish fillet, 2 to 3 minutes
- Frozen fish fillet, 3 to 4 minutes
- Fresh fish steak, 3 to 4 minutes
- Frozen fish steak, 4 to 6 minutes
- Fresh lobster, 3 to 4 minutes
- Frozen lobster, 4 to 6 minutes
- Fresh Mussels, 2 to 3 minutes
- Seafood soup or fish stock, 7 to 8 minutes
- Fresh Shrimp or Prawns, 1 to 3 minutes
- Frozen Shrimp or Prawns, 2 to 4 minutes

Rice and Grains – Cooking Time Guidelines
- Pearl barley, 20 to 22 minutes
- Pot barley, 25 to 30 minutes
- Thick congee, 15 to 20 minutes
- Thin congee, 15 to 20 minutes
- Couscous, 2 to 3 minutes
- Corn, 5 to 6 minutes
- Whole Khorasan wheat, 10 to 12 minutes
- Millet, 10 to 12 minutes
- Quick oats, 2 to 3 minutes
- Steel-cut oats, 3 to 5 minutes
- Thin porridge, 10 to 15 minutes
- Quinoa, 1 minute
- Basmati rice, 4 minutes
- Brown rice, 22 to 25 minutes
- Jasmine rice, 4 minutes
- White rice, 4 minutes
- Wild rice, 20 to 25 minutes
- Sorghum, 20 to 25 minutes
- Unsoaked Spelt berries, 25 to 30 minutes
- Unsoaked Wheat berries, 20 to 25 minutes

Dried Beans, Legumes and Lentils – Cooking Time Guidelines
- Dried black beans, 20 to 25 minutes
- Soaked black beans, 4 to 5 minutes
- Dried black-eyed peas, 10 to 15 minutes
- Soaked black-eyed peas, 4 to 5 minutes
- Dried chickpeas, 35 to 40 minutes
- Soaked chickpeas, 10 to 15 minutes
- Dried cannellini beans, 30 to 35 minutes
- Soaked cannellini beans, 8 to 10 minutes
- Dried Great Northern beans, 25 to 30 minutes
- Soaked Great Northern beans, 8 to 10 minutes
- Dried red kidney beans, 25 to 30 minutes

- Soaked red kidney beans, 8 to 10 minutes
- Green lentils, 10 to 12 minutes
- Brown lentils, 10 to 12 minutes
- Red lentils, 5 to 6 minutes
- Yellow lentils, 18 to 20 minutes
- Dried lima beans, 12 to 14 minutes
- Soaked lima beans, 8 to 10 minutes
- Dried Navy beans, 20 to 25 minutes
- Soaked Navy beans, 7 to 8 minutes
- Dried Pinto beans, 25 to 30 minutes
- Soaked Pinto beans, 8 to 10 minutes
- Peas, 6 to 10 minutes
- Dried soybeans, 35 to 45 minutes
- Soaked soybeans, 18 to 20 minutes

Meat (Beef, Pork, Poultry, Lamb) – Cooking Time Guidelines
- Beef stew meat, 20 minutes
- Beef meatball, 8 to 10 minutes
- Dressed beef, 20 minutes
- Beef (brisket, pot roast, steak, rump, round, chuck, blade) small chunks, 15 minutes
- Beef ribs, 20 to 25 minutes
- Beef shanks, 25 to 30 minutes
- Beef oxtail, 40 to 50 minutes
- Boneless chicken breasts, 6 to 8 minutes
- Whole chicken (4 pounds), 8 minutes
- Bone stock chicken, 40 to 45 minutes
- Whole duck (1 pound), 10 minutes
- Ham slices, 9 to 12 minutes
- Ham shoulder (1 pound), 8 minutes
- Lamb cubes, 10 to 15 minutes
- Lamb stew meat, 12 to 15 minutes
- Lamb leg, 15 minutes
- Pork loin roast, 20 minutes
- Pork butt roast, 15 minutes
- Pork ribs, 15 to 20 minutes
- Boneless turkey breast, 7 to 9 minutes
- Whole turkey breast, 20 to 25 minutes
- Turkey drumsticks (leg), 15 to 20 minutes
- Veal chops, 5 to 8 minutes
- Veal roast, 12 minutes
- Whole quail, 8 minutes

Vegetables – Cooking Time Guidelines
- Whole artichokes, 9 to 11 minutes
- Artichoke hearts, 4 to 5 minutes
- Asparagus, 1 to 2 minutes
- Green beans, 1 to 2 minutes

- Small beetroots, 11 to 13 minutes
- Large beetroots, 20 to 25 minutes
- Broccoli florets, 1 to 2 minutes
- Broccoli stalks, 3 to 4 minutes
- Whole brussel sprouts, 2 to 3 minutes
- Shredded cabbage, 2 to 3 minutes
- Whole carrots, 6 to 8 minutes
- Cauliflower florets, 2 to 3 minutes
- Celery, 2 to 3 minutes
- Collard greens, 4 to 5 minutes
- Corn kernels, 1 to 2 minutes
- Corn on the cob, 3 to 5 minutes
- Eggplant chunks, 3 to 4 minutes
- Leeks, 2 to 3 minutes
- Okra, 2 to 3 minutes
- Parsnips chunks, 3 to 4 minutes
- Green peas, 1 to 2 minutes
- Whole baby potatoes, 8 to 10 minutes
- Small pumpkin pieces, 2 to 3 minutes
- Fresh spinach, 1 to 2 minutes
- Frozen spinach, 3 to 4 minutes
- Acorn squash slices, 6 to 7 minutes
- Butternut squash slices, 4 to 6 minutes
- Sweet potato cubes, 3 to 4 minutes
- Sweet pepper chunks, 1 to 3 minutes
- Tomato quarters, 2 to 3 minutes

Fruits – Cooking Time Guidelines
- Apple slices, 1 to 2 minutes
- Whole apples, 3 to 4 minutes
- Whole apricots or halves, 2 to 3 minutes
- Peaches, 2 to 3 minutes
- Whole pears, 3 to 4 minutes
- Plums, 2 to 3 minutes

With all this being said, let's finally dive into the 125 Weight Watchers Instant Pot recipes. I truly hope you enjoy them.

Chapter 5: Easy and Delicious Weight Watchers Instant Pot Recipes with SmartPoints

In this chapter, you will find over 120 easy and delicious Weight Watchers Smart Points recipes, which all are made by Instant Pot Pressure Cooker. Though these recipes are made by Instant Pot, you can cook them by any other similar cooking appliance, it is up to you! Hope you will have a healthy and successful Weight Watchers journey!

Pork, Beef and Lamb Recipes

1. Spicy Pork Shoulder with Sesame Pickled Cucumbers

Time: 3 hours
Servings: 10
Freestyle SmartPoints: 8
Pork Ingredients:
- 5 pounds of boneless pork shoulder, cut into 2 or 3 pieces
- 2 ½ tablespoons of garlic powder
- 2 tablespoons of brown sugar
- 1 tablespoon of crushed red pepper
- 1 tablespoon of salt
- 1 teaspoon of black pepper
- 2 tablespoons of olive oil
- ¾ cup of water

Sauce Ingredients:
- 1 tablespoon of olive oil
- 4 garlic cloves, grated
- 2 tablespoons of ginger, freshly grated
- 1/3 cup of Sriracha
- ¼ cup of low-sodium soy sauce
- 2 tablespoons of sugar-free ketchup
- 2 tablespoons of mirin
- 2 tablespoons of raw honey
- 1 tablespoon of rice wine vinegar
- 1 teaspoon of Asian fish sauce
- 1 teaspoon of sesame oil

Sesame Pickled Cucumber Ingredients:
- 6 cucumbers, thinly sliced
- 1 ½ tablespoons of rice vinegar
- 2 teaspoons of sesame oil
- 2 teaspoons of brown sugar
- ½ teaspoon of salt
- ¼ cup of red onion, thinly sliced
- 2 teaspoons of sesame seeds

Instructions:
- Season the pork shoulder with garlic powder, brown sugar, crushed red pepper, salt, and black pepper.
- Press "Saute" function on your Instant Pot and add olive oil.
- Once the oil is hot, working in batches, add the pork pieces and cook until brown on all sides, about 2 minutes per side.
- Add all the pork and ¾ cup of water to your Instant Pot.
- Lock the lid and cook at high pressure for 90 minutes.
- To make the sauce: Add the olive oil to a saucepan over medium heat. Add the garlic and ginger and cook until fragrant, about 1 to 2 minutes.
- Add the remaining sauce ingredients to the saucepan and bring to a simmer. Allow to simmer for 2 minutes or until the sauce thickens, stirring constantly. Remove from the heat and set aside.
- When the timer beeps from your Instant Pot goes off, quick release the pressure and remove the lid.
- Transfer the pork shoulder to a cutting board and shred into bite-sized pieces using a fork. Allow the pork to cool.
- While the pork is cooling, strain, and reserve the liquid from your Instant Pot.
- Prepare the sesame pickled cucumbers: In a small bowl, add all the cucumber ingredients and stir until well combined. Set aside.
- Preheat your broiler and spread the shredded pork on a rimmed baking sheet. Drizzle 2 tablespoons of the cooking liquid over the pork.
- Place the baking sheet into your broiler and broil until crispy on top.
- In a large bowl, add the pork and spicy sauce. Stir until the pork is well coated with the sauce.
- Serve and enjoy with cucumbers.

Nutrition information per serving:
- Calories: 577
- Fat: 16.8g
- Carbohydrates: 27.3g
- Dietary Fiber: 1.9g
- Protein: 77.4g

2. Gratifying Pork Tenderloin with Soy Singer Sauce

Time: 22 minutes
Servings: 6
Freestyle SmartPoints: 7
Ingredients:
- 1 (10-ounce) pork tenderloin
- 1/3 cup of low-sodium soy sauce
- 1/3 cup of water
- ¼ cup of brown sugar
- 2 tablespoons of ginger, grated
- 1 garlic clove, minced
- 1 tablespoon of sesame oil
- 2 teaspoons of cornstarch
- 1 teaspoon of salt
- 1 teaspoon of black pepper.

Instructions:
- Add the soy sauce, water, brown sugar, ginger, garlic, sesame oil, salt, and pepper in your Instant Pot. Stir until well combined.
- Add the pork tenderloin.
- Lock the lid and cook at high pressure for 5 minutes.
- When the cooking is done, naturally release the pressure and remove the lid.
- Remove the pork tenderloin and set aside.
- In a small bowl, mix the cornstarch with 2 tablespoons of water.
- Press "Saute" function on your Instant Pot and add the cornstarch mixture. Cook until the sauce thickens, stirring frequently.
- Spoon the sauce over the pork tenderloins.
- Serve and enjoy!

Nutrition information per serving:
- Calories: 240
- Fat: 7g
- Carbohydrates: 23g
- Dietary Fiber: 2g
- Protein: 21g

3. Oozing Apple Butter Pork Chops

Time: 40 minutes
Servings: 8
Freestyle SmartPoints: 6
Ingredients:
- 2 ½ pounds of boneless pork chops
- 1 teaspoon of salt
- 1 teaspoon of black pepper
- 2 tablespoons of olive oil
- 1 onion, chopped
- 3 garlic cloves, minced
- 1 (28-ounce) jar of apple butter
- 1 cup of applesauce

Instructions:
- Season the pork chops with salt and pepper
- Press "Saute" function on your Instant Pot and add the olive oil.
- Once the oil is hot, working in batches, add the pork chops and cook until brown per side. Set the cooked pork chops aside.
- Add the onions to your Instant Pot and cook until translucent, stirring occasionally.
- Add the garlic and cook for 1 minute or until fragrant, stirring constantly.
- Return the pork chops to your Instant Pot and top with applesauce and apple butter.
- Lock the lid and cook at high pressure for 20 minutes.
- When the cooking is done, naturally release the pressure and remove the lid.
- Transfer the pork chops to serving plates.
- Serve and enjoy!

Nutrition information per serving:
- Calories: 669
- Fat: 39g
- Carbohydrates: 45.3g
- Dietary Fiber: 1.9g
- Protein: 32.5g

4. Five-Star Biryani with Lamb

Time: 3 hours and 45 minutes
Servings: 6
Freestyle SmartPoints: 5
Ingredients:
- 2 pounds of lamb, cut into 1 ½-inch pieces
- 3 tablespoons of ghee
- 3 cups of onions, sliced
- 1 cup of coconut milk

- 1 cup of yogurt
- ½ teaspoon of turmeric
- 1 ½ tablespoon of prepared biryani masala
- 1 teaspoon of garam masala
- ½ teaspoon of Kashmiri chili powder
- 1 ½ teaspoon of salt
- 2 tablespoons of lemon juice
- 10 dried apricots
- 1 tablespoon of ginger, minced
- 2 tablespoons of garlic, minced
- 1 teaspoon of white poppy seeds
- ¼ cup of cilantro, chopped
- 7 mint leaves
- ¼ cup of raisins
- ¼ cup of raw cashews
- ½ cup of water
- 2 cups of basmati rice, rinsed

Instructions:
- In a blender, add ½ cup of coconut milk, ½ cup of yogurt, turmeric, biryani masala, garam masala, chili powder, salt, lemon juice, dried apricots, ginger, garlic, and white poppy seeds. Blend the mixture.
- Add the cilantro, mint, remaining coconut milk and blend until the marinade is smooth.
- In a large bowl, stir the lamb pieces with the marinade. Refrigerate for 2 to 8 hours.
- Press "Saute" function on your Instant Pot and add the ghee.
- Once the ghee has melted, add the sliced onions and cook until brown, stirring occasionally.
- Remove the onions and set aside.
- Add the raisins and cook until plump. Remove and set aside.
- Add the cashews and cook until golden brown. Remove and set aside.
- Turn off "Saute" function.
- Add half of the onions to the pot.
- Add the lamb and all the marinade to the pot. Stir until well combined.
- Lock the lid and cook at high pressure for 12 minutes.
- When the cooking is done, quick release the pressure and remove the lid.
- Add the rice to the pot.
- Lock the lid and cook at high pressure for 5 minutes.
- When the cooking is done, naturally release the pressure for 10 minutes and quick release any remaining pressure.
- Remove the lid and gently stir the biryani.
- Allow the biryani to cool for 10 minutes and sprinkle with the remaining cooked onions, raisins, and cashews.
- Serve and enjoy!

Nutrition information per serving:
- Calories: 858
- Fat: 39g
- Carbohydrates: 80g
- Dietary Fiber: 3g
- Protein: 42g

5. Astonishing Middle-Eastern Lamb Stew

Time: 1 hour and 15 minutes
Servings: 4
Freestyle SmartPoints: 2
Ingredients:
- 2 pounds of lamb stew meat shoulder, cut into 1 ½-inch pieces
- 2 tablespoons of olive oil
- 1 onion, chopped
- 6 garlic cloves, minced
- 2 tablespoons of tomato paste
- ¼ cup of apple cider vinegar
- 2 tablespoons of honey
- 1 ¼ cup of chicken stock
- 1 (15-ounce) can of chickpeas, rinsed and drained
- ¼ cup of dried apricots, chopped
- 1 teaspoon of salt
- 1 teaspoon of black pepper
- 1 teaspoon of cumin
- 1 teaspoon of ground coriander
- 1 teaspoon of turmeric
- 1 teaspoon of cinnamon
- 1 teaspoon of cumin seeds
- ½ teaspoon of chili flakes

Instructions:
- Press "Saute" function on your Instant Pot and add 2 tablespoons of olive oil.
- Once the oil is hot, add the onions and cook for 4 minutes or until fragrant.
- Add the lamb, garlic, salt, pepper, cumin, cumin seeds, ground coriander, turmeric,

cinnamon, and chili flakes. Cook for 5 minutes, stirring occasionally.
- Add the apple cider vinegar, honey, chicken stock, chickpeas, and raisins to the pot. Stir until well combined.
- Lock the lid and cook at high pressure for 50 minutes.
- When the cooking is done, naturally release the pressure and remove the lid.
- Press "Saute" function on your Instant Pot and cook until most of the liquid evaporates. Adjust the seasoning as needed. Serve and enjoy!

Nutrition information per serving:
- Calories: 563
- Fat: 22g
- Carbohydrates: 41.6g
- Dietary Fiber: 8.7g
- Protein: 49.3g

6. Grand Leg of Lamb

Time: 35 minutes
Servings: 8 to 10
Freestyle SmartPoints: 1
Ingredients:
- 1 (4-pound) boneless leg of lamb
- 2 tablespoons of avocado oil
- 2 cups of water
- 4 garlic cloves, crushed
- 2 tablespoons of rosemary, freshly chopped
- 2 tablespoons of parsley, freshly chopped
- 1 teaspoon of smoked paprika
- 1 teaspoon of onion powder
- ¼ teaspoon of red pepper flakes
- 2 teaspoons of salt
- 1 teaspoons of black pepper

Instructions:
- Season the leg of lamb with smoked paprika, onion powder, red pepper flakes, salt, and black pepper.
- Press "Saute" function on your Instant Pot and add the avocado oil.
- Once the oil is hot, add the lamb and brown on all sides.
- Turn off "Saute" function and remove the lamb.
- Spread the garlic, rosemary, and parsley over the lamb.
- Add 2 cups of water and a steam rack to your Instant Pot. Place the lamb on top of the rack.
- Lock the lid and cook at high pressure for 30 minutes.
- When the cooking is done, naturally release the pressure and remove the lid.
- Preheat your broiler and place the lamb on a broiling pan.
- Place the pan on your broiler and broil for 2 minutes or until brown on top.
- Remove and slice into strips.
- Serve and enjoy!

Nutrition information per serving:
- Calories: 432
- Fat: 25g
- Carbohydrates: 1g
- Dietary Fiber: 0.38g
- Protein: 44.7g

7. Super Yummy Mediterranean Lamb Roast with Potatoes

Time: 1 hour and 30 minutes
Servings: 12
Freestyle SmartPoints: 3
Ingredients:
- 1 (6-pound) boneless leg of lamb
- 3 pounds of potatoes, peeled and cut into 2-inch pieces
- 2 tablespoons of olive oil
- 1 teaspoon of salt
- 1 bay leaf, crushed
- ½ teaspoon of black pepper
- 1 teaspoon of marjoram
- 1 teaspoon of sage
- 3 garlic cloves, minced
- 1 teaspoon of ginger
- 1 teaspoon of thyme
- 2 cups of chicken broth
- 2 tablespoons of arrowroot powder

Instructions:
- Press "Saute" function on your Instant Pot and add the olive oil.
- Once the oil is hot, add the leg of lamb and brown on all sides. Remove and set aside.
- Season the lamb with salt, crushed bay leaf, black pepper, marjoram, sage, garlic, ginger, and thyme.

- Return the lamb to the pot and add the chicken broth.
- Lock the lid and cook at high pressure for 50 minutes.
- When the cooking is done, quick release the pressure and remove the lid.
- Add the potatoes. Lock the lid and cook at high pressure for 10 minutes.
- When the cooking is done, quick release the pressure and remove the lid.
- Check if potatoes are soft. Transfer the potatoes and lamb to a serving platter.
- Press "Saute" function on your Instant Pot to make gravy out of the chicken broth. Whisk in the arrowroot powder and cook until thickened, stirring constantly.
- Spoon the gravy over the lamb and potatoes. Serve and enjoy!

Nutrition information per serving:
- Calories: 532
- Fat: 19.3g
- Carbohydrates: 19.3g
- Dietary Fiber: 2.7g
- Protein: 66.4g

8. Full-Flavored Lamb and Winter Squash Tagine with Apricots

Time: 50 minutes
Servings: 6
Freestyle SmartPoints: 6

Ingredients:
- 1 pound of lamb shoulders, cubed
- 1 tablespoon of coconut oil
- 1 onion, chopped
- 3 garlic cloves, minced
- 1-inch fresh ginger, grated
- ½ pound of medium-sized winter squash, seeded and cubed
- 2 to 3 cups of beef stock
- ¾ cup of dried apricots
- 1 (14-ounce) can of diced tomatoes
- 1 (14-ounce) can of chickpeas
- 1 teaspoon of salt
- 1 teaspoon of black pepper

Instructions:
- Press "Saute" function on your Instant Pot and add the coconut oil.
- Once the oil is hot, add the onions and cook until brown, stirring occasionally.
- Add the cubed lamb to the Instant Pot and cook until brown on all sides.
- Add the garlic and ginger. Give a good stir.
- Add the cubed squash, beef stock, dried apricots, diced tomatoes, chickpeas, salt, and pepper to the pot.
- Lock the lid and cook at high pressure for 20 minutes.
- When the cooking is done, quick release the pressure and remove the lid.
- Serve and enjoy!

Nutrition information per serving:
- Calories: 446
- Fat: 12.4g
- Carbohydrates: 48.4g
- Dietary Fiber: 13.5g
- Protein: 36g

9. Good Tasting Pork Carnitas (Mexican Pulled Pork)

Time: 1 hour and 20 minutes
Servings: 11
Freestyle SmartPoints: 3

Ingredients:
- 2 ½ pounds of trimmed, boneless pork shoulder, cut into 4 pieces
- 2 tablespoons of olive oil
- 1 cup of chicken broth
- 3 chipotle peppers in adobo sauce
- 2 bay leaves
- 2 tablespoons of garlic powder
- ¼ teaspoon of dry adobo seasoning
- ½ teaspoon of onion powder
- 1 ½ teaspoon of cumin
- ¼ teaspoon of dry oregano
- 2 teaspoons of salt
- 1 teaspoon of black pepper

Instructions:
- Season the pork shoulder with salt and pepper.
- Press "Saute" function and add the olive to the Instant Pot.
- Once the oil is hot, add the pork pieces and cook until brown on all sides, about 5 minutes. Remove and set aside.
- Season the pork with garlic powder, cumin, oregano, and dry adobo seasoning.
- Add the chicken broth, chipotle peppers, bay leaves, and pork to the Instant Pot.

- Lock the lid and cook at high pressure for 80 minutes.
- When the cooking is done, naturally release the pressure and remove the lid.
- Transfer the pork to a cutting board and shred using two forks. Return the shredded pork to the pot and stir into the liquid.
- Remove the bay leaves and adjust the seasoning as needed.
- Serve and enjoy!

Nutrition information per serving:
- Calories: 160
- Fat: 7g
- Carbohydrates: 1g
- Dietary Fiber: 1g
- Protein: 20g

10. Magnificent Beef and Broccoli

Time: 20 minutes
Servings: 6
Freestyle SmartPoints: 3

Beef Ingredients:
- 1 ½ pound of boneless beef chuck roast, thinly sliced
- 4 cups of broccoli florets
- 2 garlic cloves, minced
- ½ teaspoon of fresh ginger, grated
- 1 teaspoon of sesame oil
- 1 teaspoon of salt
- 1 teaspoon of black pepper

Sauce Ingredients:
- 1/3 cup of low-sodium soy sauce
- 2/3 cup of beef broth
- 2 tablespoons of oyster sauce
- 3 tablespoons of brown sugar
- 1 ½ teaspoon of sesame oil
- ¼ teaspoon of red pepper chili flake

Cornstarch Ingredients:
- 2 ½ tablespoons of cornstarch plus 3 tablespoons of water

Instructions:
- Season the beef chuck roast with salt, pepper, and sesame oil.
- Press "Saute" function on your Instant Pot and add the olive to the Instant Pot.
- Once the oil is hot, add the beef and cook for 2 minutes or until brown.
- Add the garlic and ginger and cook for 1 minute or until fragrant, stirring occasionally.
- In a medium bowl, add all the sauce ingredients until well combined. Pour the sauce over the beef.
- Lock the lid and cook at high pressure for 6 minutes.
- Meanwhile, in a bowl, add the broccoli and ¼ cup of water. Microwave for 2 to 3 minutes or until the broccoli is tender.
- When the timer beeps, quick release the pressure and remove the lid.
- Press "Saute" function on your Instant Pot and stir in the cornstarch mixture.
- Add the broccoli florets and cook until the sauce has thickened, stirring occasionally. Adjust the seasoning as needed. Serve and enjoy!

Nutrition information per serving:
- Calories: 475
- Fat: 31.9g
- Carbohydrates: 12.8g
- Protein: 32.8g

11. Remarkable Cajun Chili

Time: 30 minutes
Servings: 8
Freestyle SmartPoints: 4

Ingredients:
- 2 tablespoons of olive oil
- 1 green pepper, chopped
- 1 onion, chopped
- 2 celery ribs, chopped
- 2 garlic cloves, minced
- 1 pound of ground beef
- 2 links Andouille Sausage, sliced
- 7-ounces of raw shrimp, peeled and deveined
- 1 tablespoon of parsley, freshly chopped
- 2 ½ tablespoons of Cajun seasoning
- 1 (14-ounce) can of crushed tomatoes
- 1 (14.5-ounce) can of fire roasted tomatoes
- 1 (15-ounce) can of red kidney beans, drained and rinsed
- 2 tablespoons of tomato paste
- 1 teaspoon of salt
- 2 bay leaves

Instructions:

- Press "Saute" function and add 1 tablespoon of olive oil to your Instant Pot.
- Once the oil is hot, add the green pepper, onion, celery, and garlic. Cook for 4 minutes or until softened, stirring occasionally.
- Add the remaining 1 tablespoon of olive oil and ground beef. Cook until brown, stirring frequently.
- Add the sausage and cook for 5 minutes or until brown, stirring occasionally.
- Add the shrimp and remaining ingredients to your Instant Pot. Stir until well combined.
- Lock the lid and cook at high pressure for 10 minutes.
- When the cooking is done, naturally release the pressure and remove the lid.
- Press "Saute" function on your Instant Pot and cook for 5 to 7 minutes or until the chili has thickened, stirring occasionally. Serve and enjoy!

Nutrition information per serving:
- Calories: 344
- Fat: 16.4g
- Carbohydrates: 24g
- Dietary Fiber: 6.4g
- Protein: 27.6g

12. Phenomenal Chipotle Chili

Time: 40 minutes

Servings: 4

Freestyle SmartPoints: 5

Ingredients:
- 1 pound of ground beef
- 1 tablespoon of coconut oil
- 1 large onion, finely chopped
- 6 garlic cloves, minced
- 1 teaspoon of chipotle chili powder
- 1 tablespoon of red chili powder
- 1 teaspoon of oregano
- 1 teaspoon of cumin powder
- 2 chipotle chilies in adobo sauce, roughly chopped
- 2 cups of fresh tomatoes, chopped
- 1 cup of dried kidney beans, soaked overnight
- 1 cup of water or beef broth
- 1 teaspoon of salt
- 1 teaspoon of black pepper

Topping ingredients:
- Sliced avocados
- Crushed nachos
- Lime wedges
- Sour cream
- Cilantro
- Shredded cheddar cheese

Instructions:
- Press "Saute" function on your Instant Pot and add the coconut oil.
- Once the oil is hot and ready, add the ground beef and cook until brown, stirring occasionally.
- Add the onions and garlic. Cook until softened, stirring occasionally.
- Add the remaining ingredients to your Instant Pot and stir until well combined.
- Lock the lid and cook at high pressure for 30 minutes.
- When the cooking is done, naturally release the pressure and remove the lid.
- Stir in the chili and adjust the seasoning as needed.
- Spoon the chili into serving bowls and add desired toppings. Serve and enjoy!

Nutrition information per serving:
- Calories: 459
- Fat: 26g
- Carbohydrates: 25.4g
- Protein: 28g

13. Homemade Hamburger Helper

Time: 10 minutes

Servings: 6

Freestyle SmartPoints: 7

Ingredients:
- 1 pound of ground beef
- 2 cups of beef broth
- 2 cups of elbow macaroni
- 1 cup of heavy cream
- 2 cups of shredded cheddar cheese
- ½ cup of shredded American cheese
- 1 tablespoon of onion powder
- 1 tablespoon of garlic powder

Instructions:
- Press "Saute' function on your Instant Pot and add the ground beef and seasonings. Cook until the meat is brown, stirring occasionally.

- Add the beef broth, elbow macaroni, and heavy cream to your Instant Pot.
- Lock the lid and cook at high pressure for 4 minutes.
- When the cooking is done, quick release the pressure and remove the lid.
- Stir in the cheddar cheese and American cheese. Continue to cook and stir until all the cheese has melted.
- Serve and enjoy!

Nutrition information per serving:
- Calories: 992
- Fat: 61g
- Carbohydrates: 61g
- Dietary Fiber: 2g
- Protein: 47g

14. Famous Spaghetti

Time: 15 minutes
Servings: 6
Freestyle SmartPoints: 5
Ingredients:
- 1 pound of lean ground beef
- ½ teaspoon of salt
- ½ teaspoon of garlic powder
- ½ teaspoon of onion powder
- ½ teaspoon of Italian seasoning
- 1 pound of spaghetti noodles, break in half
- 1 (24-ounce) jar of spaghetti sauce
- 4 ½ cup of water
- 1 (14.5-ounce) can of diced tomatoes

Instructions:
- Press "Saute" function on your Instant Pot and add the ground beef.
- Add the salt, garlic powder, onion powder, and Italian seasoning. Cook until the ground beef is completely brown, stirring occasionally.
- Turn off "Saute' function on your Instant Pot and discard any excess grease from the beef if necessary.
- Add the spaghetti noodles, spaghetti sauce, water, and diced tomatoes to your Instant Pot.
- Lock the lid and cook at high pressure for 8 minutes.
- When the cooking is done, quick release the pressure and remove the lid
- Stir the spaghetti and adjust the seasoning as needed. Serve and enjoy!

Nutrition information per serving:
- Calories: 689
- Fat: 7.7g
- Carbohydrates: 116.9g
- Dietary Fiber: 4.2g
- Protein: 38.9g

15. Tempting Beef Short Ribs

Time: 1 hour and 20 minutes
Servings: 10
Freestyle SmartPoints: 9
Ingredients:
- 4 pounds of boneless beef short ribs
- 2 tablespoons of olive oil
- 1 large onion, chopped
- 2 shallots, finely chopped
- 3 garlic cloves, minced
- 3 large carrots, chopped
- 1 sprig of rosemary
- 2 sprigs of thyme, leaves removed
- 1 cup of red wine
- 1 cup of chicken broth
- 3 tablespoons of balsamic vinegar
- 2 teaspoons of salt
- 1 teaspoon of black pepper

Instructions:
- Season the ribs with salt and pepper.
- Press "Saute" function on your Instant Pot and add 1 tablespoon of olive oil.
- Add the ribs to your Instant Pot and sear for 6 to 8 minutes.
- Flip the ribs and cook for 5 minutes or until brown.
- Once the meat is brown, transfer to a plate and add the remaining tablespoon of olive oil.
- Add the onions, shallots, garlic, and carrots to your Instant Pot and cook until soft.
- Add the red wine, chicken broth, and balsamic vinegar to your Instant Pot. Stir until well combined.
- Return the beef short ribs to your Instant Pot and top with rosemary.
- Lock the lid and cook at high pressure for 45 minutes.
- When the cooking is done, naturally release the pressure and remove the lid.
- Transfer the ribs to a serving platter.
- Press "Saute" function and bring the broth to a boil. Cook until half of the liquid has

reduced and thickened, stirring occasionally. Sprinkle with thyme leaves

- Pour the sauce over the ribs. Serve and enjoy!

Nutrition information per serving:

- Calories: 407
- Fat: 14.3g
- Carbohydrates: 5.9g
- Dietary Fiber: 0.9g
- Protein: 56.2g

Chicken, Turkey and Duck Recipes

1. Charming Chicken Adobo

Time: 1 hour and 20 minutes
Servings: 4
Freestyle SmartPoints: 3
Ingredients:
- 4 chicken legs
- 2 tablespoons of olive oil
- 1/3 cup of soy sauce
- ¼ cup of white distilled vinegar
- 5 garlic cloves, crushed
- 2 bay leaves
- 1 large onion, sliced
- 2 scallions, sliced
- 1 teaspoon of salt
- 1 teaspoon of black pepper

Instructions:
- Press "Saute" function on your Instant Pot and add the olive oil.
- *Once the oil is hot, working in batches, add the chicken and cook for 4 minutes per side until brown.*
- Remove the chicken and set aside.
- Stir in the soy sauce, white vinegar, garlic, bay leaves, onion, salt, and pepper. Add the chicken to the pot.
- Lock the lid and cook at high pressure for 8 minutes.
- When the cooking is done, quick release the pressure and remove the lid.
- Press "Saute" function and bring the sauce to a boil. Cook for about 20 minutes or until the sauce is dark brown and fragrant. Remove the bay leaves.
- Transfer the chicken to a plate and spoon the sauce over.
- Sprinkle with scallions.
- Serve and enjoy!

Nutrition information per serving:
- Calories: 372
- Fat: 17.9g
- Carbohydrates: 6.5g
- Dietary Fiber: 1.1g
- Protein: 44.2g

2. Creamy Garlic Tuscan Chicken Thighs

Time: 35 minutes
Servings: 4
Freestyle SmartPoints: 6
Ingredients:
- 4 chicken thighs
- 4-ounces of cream cheese
- 2 ½ cups of fresh spinach
- ¼ cup of sundried tomatoes
- ¼ cup of Parmigiano-Reggiano, grated
- 3 garlic cloves, minced
- 1 tablespoon of olive oil
- 1 cup of chicken broth
- 1 cup of heavy cream
- 2 tablespoons of heavy whipping cream
- 2 teaspoons of Italian seasoning
- 1 teaspoon of salt
- 1 teaspoon of black pepper
- 1 teaspoon of cornstarch

Instructions:
- Season the chicken thighs with the Italian seasoning, salt, and pepper.
- Press "Saute" function on your Instant Pot and add the olive oil.
- Once the oil is hot, add the chicken and cook for 3 minutes per side or until brown.
- Add the chicken broth and heavy cream to your Instant Pot.
- Lock the lid and cook at high pressure for 14 minutes.
- When the cooking is done, quick release the pressure and remove the lid.
- Add the sundried tomatoes, cream cheese, whipping cream, grated cheese, garlic, and spinach in your Instant Pot.
- Press "Saute" function and cook for 4 minutes or until the cheese has melted and the spinach has wilted, stirring occasionally.
- In a small bowl, add the cornstarch and a little bit of water. Stir well and add to the pot.
- Cook until the sauce thickens, stirring occasionally. Serve and enjoy!

Nutrition information per serving:
- Calories: 226
- Fat: 14g
- Carbohydrates: 9.2g
- Dietary Fiber: 3g
- Protein: 17g

3. Desirable White Chicken Chili

Time: 1 hour
Servings: 6
Freestyle SmartPoints: 2
Ingredients:
- 2 tablespoons of butter
- 1 medium onion, chopped
- 10 medium boneless, skinless chicken thighs, cut into bite-sized pieces
- 1 pound of cauliflower, chopped into florets
- 4 cups of chicken stock
- 2 cups of sour cream
- 1 cup of heavy whipping cream
- 1 (14-ounce) can of diced green chiles
- 2 teaspoons of salt
- 2 teaspoons of cumin
- 2 teaspoons of oregano
- 1 teaspoon of black pepper

Instructions:
- Press "Saute" function on your Instant Pot and add the butter.
- Once the butter has melted, add the onions and chicken. Cook until the chicken is brown, stirring occasionally.
- Add the green chiles, salt, cumin, oregano, black pepper, and cauliflower. Stir until well combined.
- Add the 4 cups of chicken stock.
- Lock the lid and cook at high pressure for 30 minutes.
- When the cooking is done, naturally release the pressure for 10 minutes and remove the lid.
- In a bowl, stir in the sour cream and heavy whipping cream. Add to your pot.
- Serve and enjoy!

Nutrition information per serving:
- Calories: 523
- Fat: 32g
- Carbohydrates: 12g
- Dietary Fiber: 3.5g
- Protein: 41.5g

4. Rich Honey Teriyaki Chicken

Time: 45 minutes
Servings: 6
Freestyle SmartPoints: 7
Chicken Ingredients:
- 6 to 8 chicken thighs
- 1 tablespoon of olive oil
- 1 green onion, sliced
- Sesame seeds, for garnish

Honey Teriyaki Sauce Ingredients:
- ½ cup of low-sodium soy sauce
- ¼ cup of rice vinegar
- 2 garlic cloves, minced
- 1 tablespoon of olive oil
- 2 teaspoons of ginger, freshly grated
- 2 tablespoons of honey
- 1 tablespoon of cornstarch
- 1 teaspoon of salt
- ½ teaspoon of black pepper

Instructions:
- In a medium bowl, add all the honey teriyaki sauce ingredients and stir until well combined. Set aside.
- Press "Saute" function on your Instant Pot and add the olive oil.
- Once the oil is hot, add the chicken thighs and cook for 2 to 3 minutes per side.
- Add the teriyaki sauce. Lock the lid and cook at high pressure for 20 minutes.
- When the cooking is done, naturally release the pressure and remove the lid.
- Transfer the chicken to serving plates and sprinkle sliced green onions and sesame seeds.
- Serve and enjoy!

Nutrition information per serving:
- Calories: 200
- Fat: 9g
- Carbohydrates: 9g
- Dietary Fiber: 0g
- Protein: 22g

5. Enchanting Chicken Cacciatore

Time: 35 minutes
Servings: 6
Freestyle SmartPoints: 5
Ingredients:
- 1 ½ pounds of boneless, skinless chicken thighs
- 2 boneless, skinless chicken breasts
- 1 red bell pepper, seeded and sliced into thin strips
- ½ onion, chopped
- 3 garlic cloves, minced
- ½ cup of dry white wine

- ½ cup of chicken broth
- 1 (28-ounce) can of diced tomatoes, undrained
- 3 tablespoons of capers
- 3 sprigs fresh oregano
- 4 sprigs of fresh basil
- ½ cup of flour
- 2 tablespoons of olive oil
- 1 teaspoon of salt
- 1 teaspoon of black pepper

Instructions:
- Coat the chicken thighs with the flour.
- Press "Saute" function on your Instant Pot and add the olive oil.
- Once the oil is hot, add the chicken thighs and cook on both sides until no longer pink. Remove and set aside.
- Add the onion, garlic, bell pepper, white wine, chicken broth, capers, tomatoes, and herbs to your Instant Pot.
- Add the chicken thighs and chicken breasts to the pot.
- Lock the lid and cook at high pressure for 10 minutes.
- When the cooking is done, naturally release the pressure and remove the lid.
- Stir and season with salt and pepper.
- Press "Saute" function and cook until the sauce thickens, stirring occasionally.
- Serve and enjoy!

Nutrition information per serving:
- Calories: 308
- Fat: 9g
- Carbohydrates: 17g
- Dietary Fiber: 2g
- Protein: 34g

6. One of a Kind Chicken and Quinoa

Time: 30 minutes
Servings: 4
Freestyle SmartPoints: 2
Ingredients:
- 1 cup of chicken broth
- 1 cup of uncooked quinoa, rinsed
- 1 ½ pounds of boneless, skinless chicken breasts, chopped
- ½ cup of cheddar cheese, shredded
- 1 (15-ounce) can of black beans, drained and rinsed
- 1 (14.5-ounce) can of diced tomatoes, undrained
- 1 bell pepper, chopped
- ½ red onion, chopped
- 2 tablespoons of taco seasoning

Instructions:
- Add the chicken broth, quinoa, black beans, bell pepper, diced tomatoes, onions, and 1 tablespoon of taco seasoning. Stir until well combined.
- Place the chicken on top and sprinkle the remaining 1 tablespoon of taco seasoning.
- Lock the lid and cook at high pressure for 10 minutes.
- When the cooking is done, naturally release the pressure for 10 minutes and quick release the pressure.
- Sprinkle the cheddar cheese and cover the lid for 1 minute or until the cheese is melted.
- Serve and enjoy!

Nutrition information per serving:
- Calories: 509
- Fat: 14g
- Carbohydrates: 34g
- Dietary Fiber: 5g
- Protein: 52g

7. Out of This World Balsamic Chicken with Tomatoes and Greens

Time: 35 minutes
Servings: 6
Freestyle SmartPoints: 3
Ingredients:
- 2 pounds of boneless, skinless chicken thighs
- 1 bunch swiss chard
- 1 tablespoon of olive oil
- 1 large onion, thinly sliced
- 4 garlic cloves, minced
- ¼ cup of balsamic vinegar
- 1 (28-ounce) can of diced tomatoes
- 1 teaspoon of dried rosemary
- 1 teaspoon of dried thyme
- 1 teaspoon of dried basil
- 1 teaspoon of dried oregano
- 2 teaspoons of salt

- 1 teaspoon of black pepper

Instructions:
- Season the chicken thighs with 1 teaspoon of salt and black pepper.
- Strip the leaves off the Swiss chard and chop the leaves. Cut the chard stems into ½-inch pieces.
- Press "Saute" function and add the olive oil to your Instant Pot.
- When the oil is hot and ready, add the onions and cook until tender, stirring occasionally.
- Add ONLY the chard stems, chicken thighs, garlic, balsamic vinegar, diced tomatoes, and herbs in your Instant Pot. Give a good stir.
- Lock the lid and cook at high pressure for 12 minutes.
- When the cooking is done, quick release the pressure and stir in the chard leaves. Close the lead and leave it for 3 to 4 minutes or until wilted. Adjust the seasoning.
- Serve and enjoy!

Nutrition information per serving:
- Calories: 287
- Fat: 7.2g
- Carbohydrates: 8.1g
- Dietary Fiber: 2.2g
- Protein: 45.5g

8. Summer Italian Chicken

Time: 30 minutes

Servings: 8

Freestyle SmartPoints: 3

Ingredients:
- 8 boneless, skinless chicken thighs
- 2 tablespoons of avocado oil
- 1 onion, chopped
- 2 medium carrots, chopped
- ½ pounds of cremini mushrooms stemmed and quartered
- 4 garlic cloves, minced
- 1 tablespoon of tomato paste
- 2 cups of cherry tomatoes
- ½ cup of green olives pitted
- ½ cup of fresh basil leaves, thinly sliced
- ¼ cup of Italian parsley, chopped
- 1 teaspoon of salt
- 1 teaspoon of black pepper

Instructions:
- Season the chicken thighs with salt and pepper.
- Press "Saute" function on your Instant Pot and add the avocado oil.
- Once the oil is hot, add the onions, carrots, and mushrooms. Cook for 3 to 5 minutes or until the vegetables have softened.
- Stir in the garlic and tomato paste. Cook for 30 seconds or until fragrant.
- Add the chicken, cherry tomatoes, green olives. Stir until well combined.
- Lock the lid and cook at high pressure for 8 minutes.
- When the cooking is done, quick release the pressure and remove the lid.
- Stir in the basil leaves and parsley. Adjust the seasoning as needed.
- Serve and enjoy!

Nutrition information per serving:
- Calories: 318
- Fat: 11.9g
- Carbohydrates: 7.1g
- Dietary Fiber: 2g
- Protein: 44.2g

9. Delectable Chicken Enchiladas

Time: 50 minutes

Servings: 4

Freestyle SmartPoints: 3

Ingredients:
- 1 pound of boneless, skinless chicken thighs
- 2 cups of ancho chili sauce
- ½ cup of onions, chopped
- 12 corn tortillas
- 3 tablespoons of olive oil
- ½ cup of crumbled queso fresco
- 2 cups of shredded Monterey Jack cheese
- 1 teaspoon of salt
- 1 teaspoon of black pepper

Instructions:
- Add the chicken thighs and ancho chili sauce to your Instant Pot.
- Lock the lid and cook at high pressure for 10 minutes.
- When the cooking is done, naturally release the pressure for 10 minutes and quick release any remaining pressure.

- Remove the lid and transfer the chicken to a large bowl. Shred the chicken using forks. Stir in 2/3 cup of the ancho chili sauce.
- Chop the onions and put into a small bowl.
- Preheat your oven to 350 degrees Fahrenheit.
- Place tortillas on a baking sheet and lightly brush with olive oil.
- Place inside your oven and bake for 3 minutes or until warm. Remove from the oven.
- Spoon ½ cup of the warm ancho chili sauce into a baking dish.
- Working one-by-one, lightly coat each tortilla with the sauce and generously add the shredded chicken and onions on the tortilla.
- Sprinkle shredded Monterey Jack cheese over the chicken and onion.
- Wrap the tortilla and repeat until all the tortillas are used up.
- Once all the tortillas are prepared, generously pour leftover ancho chili sauce over them and sprinkle remaining cheese over the enchiladas.
- Place inside your oven and bake for 8 to 10 minutes or until warmed through.
- Sprinkle crumbled queso fresco over the enchiladas. Serve and enjoy!

Nutrition information per serving:
- Calories: 695
- Fat: 38g
- Carbohydrates: 67g
- Protein: 51g

10. Finger Licking Chicken Marsala

Time: 40 minutes
Servings: 4
Freestyle SmartPoints: 4
Ingredients:
- 5 boneless, skinless chicken breasts, halved or thinly sliced
- ½ cup of all-purpose flour
- 3 tablespoons of butter
- 3 tablespoons of olive oil
- 1 cup of mushrooms, stemmed and halved
- 1 shallot, thinly sliced
- 3 garlic cloves, minced
- 2/3 cup of marsala wine
- 2/3 cup of chicken stock
- ½ cup of heavy cream
- 1 teaspoon of garlic powder
- 1 teaspoon of salt
- 1 teaspoon of black pepper

Instructions:
- Add the flour on a shallow plate and dredge the chicken breasts in the flour, shake off any excess flour.
- Press "Saute" function on your Instant Pot and add the 2 tablespoons of oil and 2 tablespoons of butter.
- Once the butter is melted, working in batches, add the chicken breasts and cook on both sides until golden. Set the cooked chicken aside.
- Add the remaining tablespoons of oil and butter to your Instant Pot.
- Add the mushrooms, shallots, and garlic. Cook for 5 minutes or until tender, stirring occasionally. Season with salt and pepper.
- Add the marsala wine and chicken stock to your Instant Pot. Stir until well combined. Lay the chicken on top of the mushrooms.
- Lock the lid and cook at high pressure for 10 minutes.
- When the cooking is done, naturally release the pressure for 5 minutes and quick release any remaining pressure. Remove the lid.
- Remove the chicken and set aside.
- Press "Saute" function and stir in the heavy cream. Stir until well combined. Cook for 5 minutes or until thickened, stirring occasionally.
- Return the chicken back to the pot and stir until well coated. Serve and enjoy!

Nutrition information per serving:
- Calories: 622
- Fat: 35g
- Carbohydrates: 23g
- Dietary Fiber: 1g
- Protein: 41g

11. Award Winning Turkey Chili

Time: 18 minutes
Servings: 8
Freestyle SmartPoints: 3
Ingredients:
- 1 ½ pound of ground turkey
- 8 bacon slices, chopped
- 1 (15-ounce) can of pinto beans, rinsed and drained

- 1 (15-ounce) can of black beans, rinsed and drained
- 1 (15-ounce) can of diced tomatoes, rinsed and drained
- 1 (6-ounce) can of tomato paste
- 1 small red onion, chopped
- 1 red bell pepper, chopped
- 1 orange bell pepper, chopped
- 1 jalapeno, minced
- 2 cups of chicken stock
- 1 tablespoon of dried oregano
- 1 teaspoon of ground cumin
- 2 teaspoons of salt
- 1 teaspoon of black pepper
- 1 teaspoon of smoked paprika
- 2 tablespoons of chili powder
- 1 tablespoon of Worcestershire sauce
- 1 tablespoon of garlic, minced

Topping Ingredients:
- Sour cream
- Cilantro
- Shredded cheese

Instructions:
- Press "Saute" function on your Instant Pot and add the bacon. Cook until brown and crispy, stirring occasionally. Remove the bacon and set on a paper towel-lined plate.
- Add the onions and peppers and cook until softened, stirring occasionally.
- Add the ground turkey and cook until browned, stirring occasionally.
- Add the remaining ingredients and cooked bacon. Stir until well combined.
- Lock the lid and cook at high pressure for 18 minutes.
- When the cooking is done, naturally release the pressure for 15 minutes and quick release any remaining pressure. Remove the lid.
- Ladle the chili into serving bowls and top with desired toppings. Serve and enjoy!

Nutrition information per serving:
- Calories: 286
- Fat: 11.7g
- Carbohydrates: 19.7g
- Dietary Fiber: 6.3g
- Protein: 26.3g

12. Tantalizing Beer-And-Mustard Pulled Turkey

Time: 1 hour
Servings: 4
Freestyle SmartPoints: 6
Ingredients:
- 2 (1 ½ pound) bone-in, skinless turkey thighs
- 1 (12-ounce) bottle of dark beer
- ½ teaspoon of garlic powder
- 1 teaspoon of black pepper
- 1 teaspoon of salt
- 1 teaspoon of dry mustard
- 2 teaspoons of ground coriander
- 2 tablespoons of brown sugar
- 2 tablespoons of apple cider vinegar
- 1 tablespoon of mustard
- 1 tablespoon of canned tomato paste

Instructions:
- In a bowl, add the coriander, dry mustard, salt, black pepper, and garlic powder. Mix well.
- Rub and coat the spice mixture over the turkey thighs.
- Add the turkey thighs to your Instant Pot and add in the beer.
- Lock the lid and cook at high pressure for 45 minutes.
- When the cooking is done, quick release the pressure and remove the lid.
- Transfer the turkey thighs to a plate and shred using forks. Set aside.
- Press "Saute" function on your Instant Pot and allow the liquid to simmer until reduced to about half.
- Stir in the brown sugar, apple cider vinegar, mustard, and tomato paste until smooth. Cook for 1 minute, stirring occasionally.
- Return the turkey and give a good stir.

Nutrition information per serving:
- Calories: 406
- Fat: 20.1g
- Carbohydrates: 3g
- Dietary Fiber: 0g
- Protein: 44.7g

13. Extraordinary Honey Garlic Chicken

Time: 25 minutes

Servings: 4

Freestyle SmartPoints: 9

Ingredients:
- 4 to 6 bone-in, skinless chicken thighs
- 1/3 cup of honey
- 4 garlic cloves, minced
- ½ cup of low-sodium soy sauce
- ½ cup of sugar-free ketchup
- ½ teaspoon of dried oregano
- 2 tablespoons of parsley, chopped
- 1 tablespoon of sesame seed oil
- 1 teaspoon of salt
- 1 teaspoon of black pepper
- ½ tablespoon of toasted sesame seeds, for garnish

Instructions:
- In a bowl, add the honey, garlic, soy sauce, ketchup, oregano, and parsley Mix until well combined and set aside.
- Season the chicken thighs with salt and pepper.
- Press "Saute" function and add the sesame oil.
- Once the oil is hot, add the chicken thighs and cook for 3 minutes on both sides.
- Add the honey garlic sauce to your Instant Pot.
- Lock the lid and cook at high pressure for 20 minutes.
- When the cooking is done, naturally release the pressure for 5 minutes and quick release any remaining pressure.
- Transfer the chicken to serving plate and spoon the sauce over. Serve and enjoy!

Nutrition information per serving:
- Calories: 360
- Fat: 10g
- Carbohydrates: 35g
- Dietary Fiber: 6g
- Protein: 32g

14. Refreshing Duck Confit

Time: 2 hours

Servings: 4

Freestyle SmartPoints: 3

Ingredients:
- 4 duck legs
- 2 tablespoons of olive oil
- 1 tablespoon of salt
- 4 sprigs fresh thyme
- 4 garlic cloves, crushed
- 2 bay leaves, torn in half
- ¼ teaspoon of black peppercorns, crushed
- ¼ teaspoon of allspice berries, crushed

Instructions:
- Season the duck legs with salt, bay leaves, peppercorns, and allspice.
- Press "Saute" function on your Instant Pot and add the olive oil.
- Once the oil is hot, add the duck legs and cook until golden brown on both sides.
- Add the garlic and thyme on top of the duck.
- Lock the lid and cook at high pressure for 40 minutes. You don't need to add any additional liquid as the duck legs contain enough moisture to create steam.
- When the timer beeps, quick release the pressure and remove the lid. Flip the duck legs over.
- Lock the lid and cook at high pressure for 30 minutes.
- When the cooking is done, naturally release the pressure and remove the lid.
- Remove the duck legs and allow to cool.
- Serve and enjoy!

Nutrition information per serving:
- Calories: 194
- Fat: 11.5g
- Carbohydrates: 0g
- Dietary Fiber: 0g
- Protein: 21.8g

15. Exquisite Orange Duck and Gravy

Time: 1 hour and 30 minutes

Servings: 4

Freestyle SmartPoints: 5

Ingredients:
- 4 duck legs
- 2 tablespoons of avocado oil
- 1 yellow onion, chopped
- 1 celery rib, chopped
- 1 large carrot, chopped
- 8 garlic cloves, crushed

- 1 tablespoon of tomato paste
- ½ cup of chicken stock
- 1 teaspoon of orange zest
- ¼ cup of orange juice
- 2 tablespoons of Italian parsley, chopped
- 1 dried bay leaf
- 1 fresh thyme sprig
- ½ teaspoon of herbes de Provence
- 1 teaspoon of salt
- 1 teaspoon of black pepper

Instructions:

- In a small bowl, add the salt, black pepper, and herbes de Provence. Mix well.
- Sprinkle the seasonings over the duck legs.
- Press "Saute" function on your Instant Pot and add 1 tablespoon of avocado oil.
- Add the onions, celery, and carrots. Cook for 3 to 5 minutes or until the vegetables has softened, stirring occasionally.
- Add the garlic cloves and tomato paste. Cook for 30 seconds or until fragrant, stirring occasionally. Pour in the chicken stock to the pot.
- Stir in the orange juice, orange zest, parsley, bay leaf, and thyme. Turn off "Saute" function. Place the seasoned dug legs on top of the vegetables.
- Lock the lid and cook at high pressure for 45 minutes.
- When the cooking is done, naturally release the pressure for 20 minutes and remove the lid.
- Carefully remove the duck legs and discard the thyme sprig and bay leaf.
- Use an immersion blender to puree the contents of the Instant Pot until smooth and thick. Adjust the seasoning as needed.
- Heat a large cast-iron skillet over medium-high heat. Once the skillet is hot, add 1 tablespoon of avocado oil and duck legs. Cook for 2 to 3 minutes on both sides or until golden brown and crispy.
- Place the duck legs onto serving plates and spoon the gravy over. Serve!

Nutrition information per serving: Calories: 183, Fat: 5.6g, Carbohydrates: 9.5g, Dietary Fiber: 1.8g, Protein: 23.2g

Fish and Seafood Recipes

1. Well-Done Seafood Gumbo

Time: 10 minutes

Servings: 8

Freestyle SmartPoints: 6

Ingredients:
- 2-pounds of medium or large raw shrimp, peeled and deveined
- 24-ounces of sea bass fillets patted dry and cut into 2-inch pieces
- 3 tablespoons of ghee
- 3 tablespoons of Cajun or Creole seasoning
- 2 yellow onions, chopped
- 2 bell peppers, chopped
- 4 celery ribs, chopped
- 1 (28-ounce) can of diced tomatoes
- ¼ cup of tomato paste
- 3 bay leaves
- 1 ½ cup of bone broth
- 1 teaspoon of salt
- 1 teaspoon of black pepper

Instructions:
- Season the bass fillets with salt, pepper and half of the Cajun seasoning.
- Press "Saute" function on your Instant Pot and add the ghee.
- Once the ghee has melted, add the fish and cook for 4 minutes or until it looks cooked. Transfer the fish to a large plate.
- Add the onions, bell pepper, celery, and rest of the Cajun seasoning to your Instant Pot. Cook for 2 minutes or until fragrant, stirring occasionally.
- Turn off "Saute" function on your Instant Pot.
- Add the cooked fish, diced tomatoes, tomato paste, bay leaves and bone broth to your Instant Pot. Stir well.
- Lock the lid and cook at high pressure for 5 minutes.
- When the cooking is done, quick release the pressure and remove the lid. Discard the bay leaves.
- Press "Saute" function again and add the shrimp to your Instant Pot. Cook for 4 minutes or until the shrimp becomes opaque.
- Adjust the seasoning as needed. Serve and enjoy!

Nutrition information per serving:
- Calories: 327
- Fat: 9.2g
- Carbohydrates: 12g
- Protein: 47.8g

2. Louisiana-Style Seafood Chicken, and Sausage Gumbo

Time: 1 hour

Servings: 6

Freestyle SmartPoints: 7

Gumbo Ingredients:
- 2 (6-ounce) boneless, skinless chicken breasts
- 1 pound of raw shrimp, peeled and deveined
- 1 cup chicken andouille sausage link, sliced into pieces
- 1 cup of green bell peppers, chopped
- 1 cup of celery, chopped
- 1 cup of yellow onions, chopped
- 2 cups of frozen okra, chopped
- 1 (14.5-ounce) can of crushed tomatoes
- 1 tablespoon of garlic, minced
- 2 cups of chicken stock
- 2 tablespoons of olive oil
- 4 tablespoons of butter

Seasoning Ingredients:
- 1 bay leaf
- 1 teaspoon of ground basil
- 1 teaspoon of cayenne pepper
- 1 teaspoon of oregano
- 1 tablespoon of Creole seasoning
- ½ teaspoon of thyme
- 1 tablespoon of Worcestershire sauce

Instructions:
- Press "Saute" function and add 1 tablespoon of olive oil to your Instant Pot.
- Add the chicken sausage and cook for 2 to 3 minutes or until brown. Remove the chicken sausage and set aside. Add the butter and remaining tablespoon of olive oil to your Instant Pot.
- Add the green peppers, celery, and onions to your Instant Pot. Cook for 3 minutes or until softened, stirring occasionally.

- Add all the seasonings, garlic, and Worcestershire sauce to your Instant Pot. Give a good stir.
- Add the chicken stock, diced tomatoes, and okra.
- Add the chicken sausage and chicken breast to your Instant Pot.
- Lock the lid and cook at high pressure for 15 minutes.
- When the cooking is done, naturally release the pressure for 10 minutes and quick release any remaining pressure.
- Remove the chicken from your Instant Pot and shred using two forks. Return the shredded chicken to your Instant Pot. Press "Saute" function and add the raw shrimp to the pot.
- Cook for 3 to 5 minutes or until the shrimp turns pink. Adjust the seasoning as needed.
- Serve and enjoy!

Nutrition information per serving:
- Calories: 344
- Fat: 16.6g
- Carbohydrates: 11.3g
- Dietary Fiber: 2.9g
- Protein: 36.7g

3. Thai Coconut Clams

Time: 30 minutes
Servings: 6
Freestyle SmartPoints: 2
Ingredients:
- 3 shallots, sliced
- 1 tablespoon of coconut oil
- 1 stalk fresh lemongrass, peeled, smashed and minced
- ½ cup of vegetable broth
- 1 (1-inch) piece of fresh ginger, minced
- 2 jalapeno peppers, seeded and sliced
- 2 tablespoons of Asian fish sauce
- 1 tablespoon of light brown sugar
- ½ cup of low-fat coconut milk
- 2 pounds of clams, scrubbed
- 1 teaspoon of salt
- 1 teaspoon of black pepper
- 1 scallion, chopped
- ½ cup of fresh cilantro, chopped
- 1 lime, juiced

Instructions:
- Press "Saute" function and add the coconut oil to your Instant Pot.
- Once the oil is hot, add the shallots and cook for 3 to 5 minutes or until browned, stirring occasionally.
- Add the lemongrass, stock, ginger, jalapenos, fish sauce, and brown sugar. Allow simmering for 1 minute or until the brown sugar dissolves.
- Stir in the coconut milk and allow to simmer until thickened, about 5 minutes.
- Stir in the clams, salt, and black pepper. Close and lock the lid and cook at low pressure for 1 minute.
- When the cooking is done, naturally release the pressure and remove the lid.
- Spoon the clams into serving bowls and ladle some broth over them.
- Garnish with scallions, cilantro, and fresh lime juice. Serve and enjoy!

Nutrition information per serving:
- Calories: 343
- Fat: 12g
- Carbohydrates: 17g
- Dietary Fiber: 3g
- Protein: 36g

4. Classy Coconut Curry Sea Bass

Time: 20 minutes
Servings: 3
Freestyle SmartPoints: 6
Ingredients:
- 1 pound of sea bass, cut into 1-inch pieces
- 1 (14.5-ounce) can of coconut milk
- 1 lime, juice
- 1 tablespoon of red curry paste
- 1 teaspoon of fish sauce
- 1 teaspoon of coconut aminos
- 1 teaspoon of honey
- 2 teaspoons of Sriracha
- 2 garlic cloves, minced
- 1 teaspoon of ground turmeric
- 1 teaspoon of ground ginger
- ½ teaspoon of salt
- ½ teaspoon of white pepper
- ¼ cup of cilantro, freshly chopped
- 3 lime wedges

Instructions:

- Add the coconut milk, red curry paste, fish sauce, coconut aminos, honey, sriracha, minced garlic, ground turmeric, ground ginger, salt, and pepper in your Instant Pot. Whisk until well combined.
- Place the sea bass in your Instant Pot and spoon the coconut milk mixture over.
- Lock the lid and cook at high pressure for 3 minutes.
- When the cooking is done, quick release the pressure and remove the lid.
- Transfer the fish and broth to serving bowls.
- Garnish with cilantro and lime wedges.
- Serve and enjoy!

Nutrition information per serving:
- Calories: 413
- Fat: 35.7g
- Carbohydrates: 11g
- Dietary Fiber: 3.7g
- Protein: 16.8g

5. Enjoyable Shrimp Paella

Time: 15 minutes
Servings: 4
Freestyle SmartPoints: 4
Ingredients:
- 1 pound of frozen jumbo shrimp, shell and tails on
- 1 cup of jasmine rice
- 4 tablespoons of butter
- 1 onion, chopped
- 4 garlic cloves, minced
- 1 red pepper, chopped
- 1 cup of chicken stock
- ½ cup of white wine
- 1 teaspoon of paprika
- 1 teaspoon of turmeric
- ½ teaspoon of salt
- ¼ teaspoon of black pepper
- 1 pinch of saffron threads
- ¼ teaspoon of red pepper flakes
- ¼ cup of cilantro, chopped

Instructions:
- Press "Saute" function on your Instant Pot and add the butter.
- Once the butter has melted, add the onions and cook until softened.
- Add the garlic and cook for 1 minute or until fragrant, stirring occasionally.
- Add the paprika, turmeric, red pepper flakes, saffron threads, salt, and black pepper. Stir and cook for 1 minute.
- Add the red peppers and rice. Stir and cook for 30 seconds.
- Pour in the chicken stock and white wine. Place the shrimp on top.
- Lock the lid and cook at high pressure for 5 minutes.
- When the cooking is done, quick release the pressure and remove the lid.
- Remove the shrimp and peel.
- Spoon the rice into serving bowls and place shrimp on top.
- Serve and enjoy!

Nutrition information per serving:
- Calories: 318
- Fat: 13.2g
- Carbohydrates: 45g
- Dietary Fiber: 2.1g
- Protein: 26.4g

6. Generous Salmon with Chili-Lime Sauce

Time: 15 minutes
Servings: 2
Freestyle SmartPoints: 3
Salmon Ingredients:
- 2 95-ounce) salmon fillets
- 1 cup of water
- 1 teaspoon of salt
- 1 teaspoon of black pepper

Chili-Lime Sauce Ingredients:
- 1 jalapeno, seeded and chopped
- 1 lime, juiced
- 2 garlic cloves, minced
- 1 tablespoon of honey
- 1 tablespoon of olive oil
- 1 tablespoon of water
- 1 tablespoon of parsley, freshly chopped
- ½ teaspoon of paprika
- ½ teaspoon of cumin

Instructions:
- In a bowl, add all the chili-lime sauce ingredients. Mix until well combined.

- Add 1 cup of water and a steam rack inside your Instant Pot.
- Season your salmon fillets with salt and pepper.
- Place the salmon fillets on top of the steam rack.
- Lock the lid and cook at high pressure for 5 minutes.
- When the cooking is done, quick release the pressure and remove the lid.
- Drizzle the salmon fillets with the chili-lime sauce.
- Serve and enjoy!

Nutrition information per serving:
- Calories: 400
- Fat: 25g
- Carbohydrates: 10.5g
- Dietary Fiber: 0.5g
- Protein: 29g

7. Finger Licking Coconut Fish Curry

Time: 20 minutes

Servings: 6

Freestyle SmartPoints: 6

Ingredients:
- 1 ½ pounds of fish fillets, cut into bite-sized pieces
- 1 tomato, chopped
- 2 green chilis, sliced
- 2 garlic cloves, crushed
- 1 tablespoon of olive oil
- 1 tablespoon of ginger, freshly grated
- 6 curry leaves
- 1 tablespoon of ground coriander
- 2 teaspoons of ground cumin
- ½ teaspoon of ground turmeric
- 1 teaspoon of chili powder
- ½ teaspoon of ground fenugreek
- 3 tablespoon of curry powder
- 2 cups of unsweetened coconut milk
- 2 teaspoons of salt
- ½ lemon, squeezed

Instructions:
- Press "Saute" function on your Instant Pot and add the olive oil.
- Add the curry leaves and allow to simmer until golden around the edges.
- Add the onions, garlic, and ginger. Cook until the onions have softened, stirring occasionally.
- Add the coriander, cumin, turmeric, chili powder and fenugreek and cook for 2 minutes or until the aroma is released.
- Stir in the coconut milk, green chilis, tomatoes and fish pieces.
- Lock the lid and cook at low pressure for 5 minutes.
- When the cooking is done, naturally release the pressure and remove the lid.
- Season with salt and squeeze the lemon.
- Serve and enjoy!

Nutrition information per serving:
- Calories: 474
- Fat: 35.3g
- Carbohydrates: 25g
- Dietary Fiber: 2.6g
- Protein: 18.7g

8. Gorgeous Lemon-Shrimp Risotto with Vegetables and Parmesan

Time: 25 minutes

Servings: 4

Freestyle SmartPoints: 4

Ingredients:
- 1 ½ cup of Arborio rice
- 1 pound of shrimp, peeled and deveined
- ½ cup of Parmigiano-Reggiano, shredded
- 2 teaspoons of olive oil
- 1 cup of fresh spinach
- 1 bunch of asparagus, sliced
- 3 ½ cup of chicken stock
- ½ cup of dry white wine
- 3 garlic cloves, minced
- ½ white onion, chopped
- 1 tablespoon of parsley, chopped
- ½ lemon, juiced
- 1 tablespoon of butter
- 1 teaspoon of salt
- 1 teaspoon of black pepper

Instructions:
- Press "Saute" function on your Instant Pot and add the olive oil.
- Once the oil is hot and ready, add the asparagus and cook for 3 minutes or until

softened, stirring constantly. Once done, remove the asparagus.
- Add the onions and garlic and cook until fragrant, stirring occasionally.
- Add the butter and rice to your Instant Pot. Stir for 1 to 2 minutes or until the rice is coated in butter.
- Stir in the white wine, chicken stock, and cheese. Season with salt and black pepper.
- Lock the lid and cook at high pressure for 8 minutes.
- When the cooking is done, quick release the pressure and remove the lid.
- Press "Saute" function and add the shrimp, spinach, and asparagus.
- Cook for about 4 minutes or until the shrimp is pink and the spinach has wilted, stirring occasionally.
- Turn off "Saute" function. Drizzle with fresh lemon juice and sprinkle with parsley. Serve and enjoy!

Nutrition information per serving:
- Calories: 440
- Fat: 12g
- Carbohydrates: 48g
- Dietary Fiber: 4g
- Protein: 29g

9. Nourishing Garlic Butter Salmon and Asparagus

Time: 9 minutes
Servings: 3
Freestyle SmartPoints: 4
Ingredients:
- 1 pound of salmon fillets, cut into 3 equal pieces
- 1 pound of asparagus, cut into bite-sized pieces
- ¼ cup of lemon juice
- 3 tablespoons of butter
- 1 ½ tablespoon of garlic, minced
- 1 teaspoon of salt
- ¼ teaspoon of red pepper flakes
- 2 cups of water

Instructions:
- Lay 3 large pieces of foil on a flat surface.
- Place 1 salmon piece on each foil.
- Spread ½ tablespoon of garlic on each piece of salmon.
- Divide and place the asparagus equally between the three salmon pieces.
- Sprinkle salt and red pepper flakes on top of each salmon fillet.
- Add 1 tablespoon of butter on each salmon fillet.
- Tightly wrap the foil and make sure no steam can escape.
- Add 2 cups of water and a trivet to your Instant Pot.
- Place the foil packets on top of the trivet.
- Lock the lid and press "Steam" function and set for 4 minutes.
- When the cooking is done, quick release the pressure and remove the lid.
- Remove the foil packets and unopen. Transfer the contents to a plate.
- Serve and enjoy!

Nutrition information per serving:
- Calories: 343
- Fat: 21.2g
- Carbohydrates: 8.9g
- Dietary Fiber: 3.8g
- Protein: 33.2g

10. Pleasant Fish and Potato Chowder

Time: 30 minutes
Servings: 8
Freestyle SmartPoints: 4
Ingredients:
- 2 ½ cups of fish stock or water
- 1 ½ pounds of tilapia, cut into bite-sized pieces
- 1 pound of potatoes, chopped
- 1 cup of celery, chopped
- 1 cup of onions, chopped
- 6 bacon slices, chopped
- 1 ½ cup of unsweetened coconut cream
- 3 tablespoons of butter
- ½ teaspoon of garlic powder
- 1 teaspoon of salt
- 1 teaspoon of black pepper

Instructions:
- Press "Saute" function on your Instant Pot and add the bacon. Cook the bacon until brown and crispy.
- Remove the bacon and set aside.

- Add the butter, onions, and celery. Cook until the onions have softened, stirring frequently.
- Add the fish stock, tilapia pieces, salt, pepper, garlic powder, bacon and coconut cream to your Instant Pot. Give a good stir.
- Lock the lid and cook at high pressure for 10 minutes.
- When the cooking is done, naturally release the pressure and remove the lid.
- Use a potato masher to mash the potatoes until broken down. You can leave chunks if you prefer.
- Serve and enjoy!

Nutrition information per serving:
- Calories: 348
- Fat: 22.5g
- Carbohydrates: 13.3g
- Dietary Fiber: 2.9g
- Protein: 25g

11. Soy-Free Asian Salmon

Time: 7 minutes

Servings: 2

Freestyle SmartPoints: 3

Ingredients:
- 2 salmon fillets
- 1 tablespoon of coconut oil
- 1 tablespoon of brown sugar
- 3 tablespoons of coconut aminos
- 2 tablespoons of maple syrup
- 1 tablespoon of parsley, chopped
- 1 teaspoon of paprika
- ¼ teaspoon of ginger
- 1 teaspoon of sesame seeds
- 1 teaspoon of salt
- 1 teaspoon of black pepper

Instructions:
- Press "Saute" function on your Instant Pot and add the coconut oil.
- Once the oil is hot, add the brown sugar and stir until the sugar has dissolved.
- Stir in the paprika, ginger, coconut aminos, and maple syrup.
- Add the salmon fillets to your Instant Pot and season with salt and pepper.
- Lock the lid and cook at low pressure for 2 minutes.
- When the cooking is done, naturally release the pressure for 5 minutes and quick release any remaining pressure.
- Remove the lid and transfer the salmon fillets to a plate.
- Spoon and pour some of the broth over the salmon.
- Sprinkle the fillets with sesame seeds and garnish with parsley
- Serve and enjoy!

Nutrition information per serving:
- Calories: 378
- Fat: 17.8g
- Carbohydrates: 20.8g
- Dietary Fiber: 0g
- Protein: 34.5g

12. Traditional Lemon Garlic Salmon

Time: 10 minutes

Servings: 2

Freestyle SmartPoints: 2

Ingredients:
- 1 ½ pounds of frozen salmon fillets
- ¼ cup of lemon juice
- ¾ cup of fish stock or water
- 1 lemon, thinly sliced
- 1 tablespoon of coconut oil
- 2 tablespoons of mixed herbs
- 1 teaspoon of garlic powder
- 1 teaspoon of salt
- 1 teaspoon of black pepper

Instructions:
- Add the lemon juice, fish stock, and mixed herbs to your Instant Pot.
- Place a steamer rack in Instant Pot.
- Drizzle the salmon fillets with coconut oil and season with garlic powder, salt, and black pepper.
- Place the salmon on the steamer rack and place lemon slices on top.
- Lock the lid and cook at high pressure for 7 minutes.
- When the cooking is done, quick release the pressure and remove the lid.
- Serve and enjoy!

Nutrition information per serving:
- Calories: 539
- Fat: 28.8g

- Carbohydrates: 3.3g
- Dietary Fiber: 0.9g
- Protein: 58.5g

13. Decorated Salmon, Broccoli, and Potatoes

Time: 6 minutes
Servings: 2
Freestyle SmartPoints: 2
Ingredients:
- 2 (4-ounce) salmon fillet
- 1 medium head of broccoli, chopped into florets
- 1 potato, chopped into cubes
- 1 shallot, chopped
- 2 garlic cloves, minced
- 3 tablespoons of butter
- 1 tablespoon of coconut oil
- ½ cup of fish stock
- 1 tablespoon of parsley, chopped
- 1 teaspoon of salt
- 1 teaspoon of black pepper

Instructions:
- Drizzle the coconut oil over the salmon fillet and season with salt and pepper
- Press "Saute" function on your Instant Pot and add the butter.
- Once the butter has melted, add the shallot and cook until softened, stirring occasionally.
- Add the garlic and cook for 1 minute or until fragrant.
- Add the broccoli, potatoes, and parsley to your Instant Pot. Cook for 2 minutes, stirring occasionally.
- Add ½ cup of fish stock and a steaming rack to your Instant Pot.
- Place the salmon fillets on top of the rack.
- Lock the lid and cook at high pressure for 4 minutes.
- When the cooking is done, naturally release the pressure and remove the lid.
- Transfer the salmon fillet to a plate along with the broccoli and potato mixture.
- Serve and enjoy!

Nutrition information per serving:
- Calories: 467
- Fat: 31.8g
- Carbohydrates: 21.4g
- Dietary Fiber: 3.1g
- Protein: 27.1g

14. Wonderful in Taste Fish Taco Bowls

Time: 15 minutes
Servings: 4
Freestyle SmartPoints: 3
Fish Ingredients:
- 3 (6-ounce) cod fillets
- 1 tablespoon of olive oil
- ½ teaspoon of salt
- ½ teaspoon of black pepper
- 1 cup of water

Slaw Ingredients:
- ½ cup of green cabbage, grated
- 1 large carrot, peeled and grated
- 2 tablespoons of fresh orange juice
- 2 dashes of sriracha sauce
- ¼ cup of cilantro, freshly chopped
- ¼ cup of low-fat mayonnaise
- 1 medium avocado, peeled and diced
- 2 Roma tomatoes, chopped
- ½ large lime, juice
- 1 teaspoon of ground cumin
- 1 teaspoon of garlic salt

Instructions:
- In a large bowl, add all the slaw ingredients and stir until well combined.
- Add 1 cup of water and a trivet to your Instant Pot.
- Place a steamer basket on top of the trivet.
- Season the cod fillets with salt and pepper and drizzle olive oil.
- Place the cod fillets onto steamer basket.
- Lock the lid and cook at high pressure for 3 minutes.
- When the cooking is done, quick release the pressure and remove the lid.
- Distribute the slaw into serving bowls and add the cod fillet.
- Serve and enjoy!

Nutrition information per serving:
- Calories: 284
- Fat: 19.1g
- Carbohydrates: 13.4g
- Dietary Fiber: 4.8g

- Protein: 17g

15. Wholesome Clam Chowder

Time: 30 minutes

Servings: 6

Freestyle SmartPoints: 5

Ingredients:
- 3 (6.5-ounce) cans of chopped clams, juice reserved
- 4 slices of bacon, chopped
- 3 tablespoons of butter
- 1 onion, chopped
- 2 celery stalks, chopped
- 1 ½ pounds of potatoes, chopped
- 1 1/3 cup of heavy cream
- 1 tablespoon of cornstarch
- ¼ teaspoon of dried thyme
- 1 garlic clove, minced
- 1 ½ teaspoon of salt
- ¼ teaspoon of black pepper

Instructions:
- Press "Saute" function and add the chopped bacon to your Instant Pot. Cook the bacon until no more fat, but not crispy.
- Add the butter, onion, celery, and thyme. Cook for 4 minutes or until the onions are translucent, stirring occasionally.
- Add the garlic, salt, and black pepper. Cook for 1 minute or until fragrant, stirring frequently.
- Stir in the potatoes and clam juice.
- Lock the lid and cook at high pressure for 5 minutes.
- When the cooking is done, quick release the pressure and remove the lid.
- Use a potato masher and mash the potatoes.
- Press" Saute" function and stir in the clams and heavy cream.
- Add the cornstarch and cook until thickened. Adjust the seasoning as needed.
- Serve and enjoy!

Nutrition information per serving:
- Calories: 386
- Fat: 25.7g
- Carbohydrates: 32.7g
- Dietary Fiber: 4.9g
- Protein: 8.8g

Vegan and Vegetarian Recipes

1. Legendary Artichokes

Time: 18 minutes

Servings: 3

Freestyle SmartPoints: 2

Ingredients:
- 3 medium-sized artichokes
- ½ cup of sour cream
- 3 tablespoons of mayonnaise
- 1 teaspoon of minced garlic
- 1 teaspoon of salt
- 1 teaspoon of dill
- 2 tablespoons of grated parmesan cheese

Instructions:
- Remove the tops of your artichokes.
- Add 1 cup of water and a vegetable steamer to your Instant Pot.
- Put the 3 artichokes in the vegetable steamer.
- Sprinkle the artichokes with salt.
- Lock the lid and cook at high pressure for 8 minutes.
- When the cooking is done, quick release the pressure and remove the lid.
- Sprinkle the artichokes with the parmesan cheese.
- In a bowl, add the sour cream, mayonnaise, garlic, and dill. Mix well.
- Serve and enjoy the dip.

Nutrition information per serving:
- Calories: 245
- Fat: 19g
- Carbohydrates: 15g
- Dietary Fiber: 6g
- Protein: 6g

2. Dazzling Jackfruit Curry

Time: 1 hour

Servings: 2

Freestyle SmartPoints: 4

Ingredients:
- 1 small onion, chopped
- 1-inch ginger, chopped or grated
- 5 garlic cloves, minced
- 1 ½ cup of pureed tomatoes
- 1 (20-ounce) can of green Jackfruit, drained and rinsed
- 1 teaspoon of coconut oil
- 1 teaspoon of coriander powder
- ½ teaspoon of turmeric
- ¼ teaspoon of black pepper
- ½ teaspoon of salt
- ½ teaspoon of cumin seeds
- ½ teaspoon of mustard seeds
- ½ teaspoon of nigella seeds
- 2 bay leaves
- 2 dried red chilies
- 1 to 1 ½ cup of vegetable stock

Instructions:
- Press "Saute" function on your Instant Pot and add the coconut oil.
- Once the oil is hot, add the cumin, mustard and nigella seeds. Cook for 1 minute, stirring constantly.
- Add the bay leaves and red chilies and cook for only a few seconds, stirring constantly.
- Add the onion, garlic, and ginger and cook for 5 minutes or until translucent, stirring occasionally.
- Add the coriander, turmeric, black pepper and stir well.
- Add the pureed tomato, salt, and Jackfruit to your Instant Pot and stir until well combined.
- Add the vegetable stock to your Instant Pot.
- Lock the lid and cook at high pressure for 7 minutes.
- When the cooking is done, naturally release the pressure and remove the lid.
- Shred the jackfruit using a spatula if you desire. Serve and enjoy!

Nutrition information per serving:
- Calories: 369
- Fat: 3g
- Carbohydrates: 86g
- Protein: 4g

3. Deluxe Vegan Barbacoa Mushroom Tacos

Time: 30 minutes

Servings: 3

Freestyle SmartPoints: 5

Ingredients:
- 1 cup of white or cremini mushrooms, chopped

- 2 large guajillo chiles, stemmed and soaked in hot water for 15 minutes
- 1 tablespoon of olive oil
- 1 bay leaf
- 1 large onion, thinly sliced
- 7 garlic cloves, minced
- 2 chipotle chile in adobo sauce
- 1 teaspoon of ground cumin
- ½ teaspoon of dried oregano
- ½ teaspoon of smoked hot paprika
- ¼ teaspoon of ground cinnamon
- 3 teaspoons of lime juice
- ¼ teaspoon of salt
- 1/3 cup of vegetable stock
- 1 teaspoon of apple cider vinegar

Additional Ingredients:
- Tortillas
- Avocado slices
- Salsa
- Onions
- Lime juice
- Shredded Mexican cheese

Instructions:
- Press "Saute" setting on your Instant Pot and add the olive oil.
- Once the oil is hot, add the bay leaf, onions, and garlic. Cook until translucent, stirring occasionally.
- Turn off "Saute" setting" and transfer half of the onion mixture to a blender. Add the guajillo chiles, chipotle chiles, lime juice, apple cider vinegar, and spices. Blend until smooth.
- Add the mushrooms to your Instant Pot with 1/3 cup of vegetable stock and the sauce. Stir until the mushrooms are coated with the sauce.
- Lock the lid and cook at high pressure for 5 minutes.
- When the cooking is done, naturally release the pressure for 10 minutes and quick release the remaining pressure.
- Remove the lid and remove the bay leaf.
- Add the mushrooms to tortillas with desired toppings. Serve and enjoy!

Nutrition information per serving: Calories: 176, Fat: 12g, Carbohydrates: 16g, Protein: 4g

4. The Number One Vegan Lentil Kidney Bean Chili

Time: 20 minutes
Servings: 2
Freestyle SmartPoints: 4

Ingredients:
- 1 cup of dry brown lentils, rinsed and drained
- 1 cup of kidney beans
- 1 tablespoon of olive oil
- ½ red onion, chopped
- 1 red bell pepper, chopped
- ¼ cup of celery, chopped
- 2 cups of water
- ½ cup of fresh or frozen corn
- 1 green chili, chopped
- 3 garlic cloves, minced
- 2 tomatoes, chopped
- ½ teaspoon of chipotle pepper powder
- 1 teaspoon of chili powder
- 1 teaspoon of paprika
- 1 teaspoon of salt
- 1 teaspoon of black pepper
- 1 cup of vegetable broth

Instructions:
- Press "Saute" function on your Instant Pot and add the olive oil.
- Once the oil is hot, add the onions and cook for 4 minutes or until translucent, stirring constantly.
- Add the green chili pepper and garlic and cook for 2 minutes or until fragrant, stirring occasionally.
- Add the tomatoes, chipotle pepper, seasonings and cook for 5 minutes, stirring occasionally.
- Add the bell pepper, celery and cook for an additional minute.
- Add the remaining ingredients to your Instant Pot and stir until well combined.
- Lock the lid and cook at high pressure for 7 minutes.
- Once the cooking is done, naturally release the pressure and remove the lid.
- Serve and enjoy!

Nutrition information per serving:
- Calories: 381
- Fat: 6g
- Carbohydrates: 64g
- Dietary Fiber: 24g
- Protein: 20g

5. Heavenly Eggplant Sweet Potato Lentil Curry

Time: 35 minutes
Servings: 4
Freestyle SmartPoints: 5
Ingredients:
- 1 cup of lentils, soaked in water for 15 minutes
- 2 tablespoons of olive oil
- ½ onion, chopped
- 4 garlic cloves, minced
- 1-inch ginger, grated
- 1 hot green chile, chopped
- ¼ teaspoon of turmeric
- 1 teaspoon of garam masala
- ½ teaspoon of ground cumin
- 1 (15-ounce) can of crushed tomatoes
- 1 cup of eggplants, chopped
- 1 cup of sweet potatoes, chopped
- 2 cups of vegetable broth or water
- A big handful of kale stemmed and chopped
- 1 teaspoon of salt
- 1 teaspoon of black pepper
- ¼ teaspoon of cayenne pepper

Instructions:
- Press "Saute" function on your Instant Pot and add the olive oil.
- Once the oil is hot and ready, add the onions, garlic, ginger, chile, and salt. Cook for 2 to 3 minutes, stirring frequently.
- Add the spices and stir.
- Add the tomatoes and cook for 4 minutes, stirring occasionally.
- Add the remaining ingredients except for the kale to your Instant Pot and stir until well combined.
- Lock the lid and cook at high pressure for 12 minutes.
- When the cooking is done, naturally release the pressure and remove the lid.
- Fold in the spinach and adjust the seasoning.
- Serve and enjoy!

Nutrition information per serving:
- Calories: 200
- Fat: 1g
- Carbohydrates: 35g
- Dietary Fiber: 14g
- Protein: 11.5g

6. Intriguing Vegan Red Lentil, Sweet Potato, Hemp Burgers

Time: 40 minutes
Servings: 8
Freestyle SmartPoints: 6
Ingredients:
- 1 cup of onions, chopped
- 2 teaspoons of ginger, grated
- 1 cup of mushrooms, chopped
- 1 tablespoon of olive oil
- 1 cup of red lentils, rinsed
- 1 ½ sweet potatoes, peeled and chopped into cubes
- 2 cups of vegetable stock
- ¼ cup of hemp seeds
- ¼ cup of parsley, chopped
- ¼ cup of cilantro, chopped
- 1 tablespoon of curry powder
- 1 cup of quick oats
- 1 to 4 tablespoons of brown rice flour, if needed

Instructions:
- Press "Saute" function on your Instant Pot and add the olive oil.
- Once the oil is hot, add the onions, ginger, and mushrooms and cook for 3 minutes, stirring occasionally.
- Add the lentils, sweet potatoes, and vegetable stock.
- Lock the lid and cook at high pressure for 6 minutes.
- When the cooking is done, naturally release the pressure and remove the lid.
- Transfer the lentil mixture to a large bowl and allow to cool.
- Preheat your oven to 375 degrees Fahrenheit.
- Line a baking sheet with parchment paper and spray nonstick cooking spray.
- Use a potato masher to mash the lentil mixture.
- Stir in the hemp seeds, parsley, cilantro, curry powder, and oats. If the lentil mixture is too wet and soggy, add brown rice flour.
- Form the lentil mixture into 8 patties and place on the baking sheet.

- Place the baking sheet in your oven and bake for 10 minutes.
- Flip the burgers over and bake for an additional 10 minutes or until firm and brown. Allow cooling before putting onto hamburger buns. Serve and enjoy!

Nutrition information per serving:
- Calories: 246
- Fat: 6.5g
- Carbohydrates: 36.3g
- Dietary Fiber: 10.9g
- Protein: 11.6g

7. Lip-Smacking Mushroom Stroganoff

Time: 20 minutes
Servings: 10
Freestyle SmartPoints: 6
Ingredients:
- 1 small yellow onions, thinly sliced
- 10-ounces of cremini mushrooms, sliced
- 1 tablespoon of olive oil
- 4 cups of dry rotini pasta
- 4 cups of beef broth
- 2 tablespoons of nutritional yeast
- ¼ teaspoon of ground black pepper
- 1/3 cup of cashew butter
- 1 tablespoon of fresh lemon juice
- 1 teaspoon of salt

Instructions:
- Press "Saute" function on your Instant Pot and add the olive oil.
- Once the oil is hot, add the onions and cook for 5 minutes or until translucent.
- Add the pasta, mushrooms, broth, nutritional yeast, salt, and black pepper.
- Lock the lid and cook at high pressure for 5 minutes.
- When the cooking is done, quick release the pressure and remove the lid.
- Stir in the cashew butter and lemon juice. Adjust the seasoning as needed.
- Serve and enjoy!

Nutrition information per serving:
- Calories: 228
- Fat: 7.8g
- Carbohydrates: 31.3g
- Dietary Fiber: 1g
- Protein: 9g

8. Marvelous Vegan Black Bean Chili

Time: 40 minutes
Servings: 10
Freestyle SmartPoints: 5
Ingredients:
- 2 teaspoons of olive oil
- 2 cups of onions, chopped
- 1 red bell pepper, chopped
- 1 yellow bell pepper, chopped
- 1 teaspoon of dried oregano
- 2 garlic cloves, minced
- 2 tablespoons of chili powder
- 2 teaspoons of ground cumin
- 2 (15-ounce) cans of black beans, rinsed and drained
- 2 (14.5-ounce) cans of crushed tomatoes
- 1 medium jalapeno pepper, seeded and minced
- 1 teaspoon of salt
- 1 teaspoon of black pepper
- 1 cup of vegetable stock

Topping ingredients (optional):
- Avocado slices
- Vegan sour cream
- Lime wedges
- Crushed tortilla chips
- Chopped cilantro

Instructions:
- Press "Saute" function on your Instant Pot and add the olive oil.
- Once the oil is hot and ready, add the onions, bell pepper, and oregano. Cook for 7 minutes or until softened, stirring occasionally.
- Add the garlic, chili powder, and cumin. Cook for 1 minute, stirring constantly.
- Add the remaining ingredients to your Instant Pot and stir until well combined.
- Lock the lid and cook at high pressure for 5 minutes.
- When the cooking is done, quick release the pressure and remove the lid.
- Ladle the chili into serving bowls and add desired toppings. Serve and enjoy!

Nutrition information per serving:
- Calories: 336
- Fat: 2.7g

- Carbohydrates: 61.4g
- Dietary Fiber: 15.3g
- Protein: 19.9g

9. Indian-Inspired Pickled Potatoes

Time: 15 minutes
Servings: 4
Freestyle SmartPoints: 3
Ingredients:
- 5 potatoes, boiled and cubed
- 4 tablespoons of olive oil
- 1 bay leaf
- 5 cloves
- 1 tablespoon of coriander seeds, pounded
- 1 tablespoon of cumin seeds
- 1 tablespoon of mango pickle
- 2 teaspoons of dried fenugreek leaves
- 1 teaspoon of dry pomegranate powder
- ½ teaspoon of turmeric powder
- ½ teaspoon of red chili powder
- 1 teaspoon of salt

Instructions:
- Press "Saute" function on your Instant Pot and add 2 tablespoons of olive oil.
- Once the oil is hot, add the cumin seeds, coriander seeds, cloves, and bay leaf. Allow simmering for a few seconds.
- Add the dry spices and mix them well.
- Add the remaining 2 tablespoons of olive oil and pickle. Stir the mixture well.
- Add the potatoes and coat them with the spice mixture.
- Lock the lid and cook at high pressure for 2 minutes.
- When the cooking is done, quick release the pressure and remove the lid.
- Serve and enjoy!

Nutrition information per serving:
- Calories: 304
- Fat: 14.3g
- Carbohydrates: 41.8g
- Dietary Fiber: 6.4g
- Protein: 4.5g

10. Satisfying Vegan Quinoa Burrito Bowls

Time: 25 minutes
Servings: 4
Freestyle SmartPoints: 3
Ingredients:
- 1 teaspoon of olive oil
- ½ red onion, chopped
- 1 sweet bell pepper, chopped
- 1 cup of quinoa, rinsed well
- 1 cup of salsa
- 1 cup of water
- 1 (15-ounce) can of black beans, drained and rinsed
- ½ teaspoon of salt
- 1 teaspoon of ground cumin

Topping ingredients (optional):
- Avocado slices
- Guacamole
- Fresh cilantro
- Green onions, chopped
- Salsa
- Lime wedges
- Lettuce, shredded

Instructions:
- Press "Saute" function on your Instant Pot and add the olive oil.
- Once the oil is hot, add the onions and pepper and cook for 5 minutes or until softened, stirring constantly.
- Add the cumin and salt and cook for an additional minute.
- Turn off "Saute" function on your Instant Pot.
- Add the quinoa, salsa, water, and black beans to your Instant Pot. Stir until well combined.
- Lock the lid and cook at low pressure for 12 minutes.
- When the cooking is done, naturally release the pressure and remove the lid.
- Fluff the quinoa with a fork and spoon into serving bowls.
- Top with your desired toppings.
- Serve and enjoy!

Nutrition information per serving:
- Calories: 562
- Fat: 5.5g
- Carbohydrates: 101.2g
- Dietary Fiber: 20.9g
- Protein: 30.4g

11. Signature Curried Chickpea Stuffed Acorn Squash

Time: 30 minutes
Servings: 2
Freestyle SmartPoints: 5
Ingredients:
- 2 cups of chickpeas, soaked in water for 30 minutes
- ¼ cup of brown rice washed and soaked in water for 30 minutes
- 2 cups of vegetable stock
- 1 small acorn squash, halved and deseeded
- 1 tablespoon of olive oil
- ½ teaspoon of cumin seeds
- ½ cup of red onions, chopped
- 4 garlic cloves, minced
- ½-inch ginger, minced
- 1 green chili, minced
- ¼ teaspoon of turmeric
- ½ teaspoon of garam masala
- ½ teaspoon of dry mango powder amchur
- 2 tomatoes, chopped
- ½ teaspoon of fresh lime juice
- 1 cup of rainbow chard or spinach, chopped
- ½ teaspoon of salt
- ¼ teaspoon of cayenne pepper

Instructions:
- Add the olive oil to your Instant Pot and press "Saute" setting.
- Add the cumin seeds and cook for 1 minute or until fragrant, stirring frequently.
- Add the onions, garlic, ginger, and chili. Cook for 5 minutes or until translucent, stirring frequently.
- Add the seasoning and stir for a couple of seconds.
- Add the tomatoes, lime juice, and rainbow chard or spinach. Cook for 5 minutes, stirring occasionally.
- Add the remaining ingredients except for the acorn squash to your Instant Pot and stir until well combined.
- Place a steamer basket or a trivet to your Instant Pot and place the acorn squash on top. Lock the lid and cook at high pressure for 17 minutes.
- When the cooking is done, naturally release the pressure and remove the lid.
- Carefully remove the steamer basket and stir the chickpea rice stew.
- Fill the squash with the chickpea rice mixture. Serve and enjoy!

Nutrition information per serving:
- Calories: 518
- Fat: 8g
- Carbohydrates: 97g
- Protein: 20g

12. Terrific Vegan Sloppy Joes

Time: 30 minutes
Servings: 8
Freestyle SmartPoints: 3
Ingredients:
- 1 cup of green/brown lentils
- 1 cup of red lentils
- 3 cups of water
- 1 large onion, chopped
- 1 red bell pepper, chopped
- 1 tablespoon of olive oil
- 2 tablespoons of apple cider vinegar
- 2 tablespoons of maple syrup
- 1 (28-ounce) can of crushed tomatoes
- 3 tablespoons of tomato paste
- 2 tablespoons of vegan Worcestershire sauce
- 1 teaspoon of salt
- 1 tablespoon of ground cumin
- 1 teaspoon of dried oregano

Instructions:
- Press "Saute" function on your Instant Pot and add the olive oil.
- Once the oil is hot, add the onion, bell pepper, and salt. Cook for 3 minutes or until softened, stirring frequently.
- Add the cumin and oregano and cook for 1 minute.
- Add the tomato paste and cook for 2 minutes, stirring to coat.
- Add the remaining ingredients and stir until well combined.
- Lock the lid and cook at high pressure for 13 minutes.
- When the cooking is done, allow for a natural release and remove the lid.

- Stir everything again and adjust the seasoning as needed.
- Serve over toasted hamburger buns.

Nutrition information per serving:
- Calories: 259
- Fat: 3.1g
- Carbohydrates: 47.3g
- Dietary Fiber: 5.4g
- Protein: 14.4g

13. Mexican-Style Corn on the Cob with Hemp-Lime Sauce

Time: 30 minutes
Servings: 4
Freestyle SmartPoints: 2
Ingredients:
- 4 ear corns, shucked and rinsed
- ½ cup of unsweetened coconut milk
- 2 tablespoons of hemp hearts
- 2 tablespoons of nutritional yeast
- 1 tablespoon of all-purpose flour
- 1 garlic clove, peeled
- ¼ teaspoon of cayenne pepper
- ¼ teaspoon of salt
- 1 tablespoon of fresh lime juice

Instructions:
- Place a trivet or a steaming basket inside your Instant Pot.
- Add 1 ½ cup of water and a trivet or steamer basket in your Instant Pot.
- Lock the lid and cook at high pressure for 4 minutes.
- When the cooking is done, quick release the pressure and remove the lid. Set the corn aside.
- In a blender, add the coconut milk, hemp hearts, nutritional yeast, flour, garlic, cayenne pepper, and salt. Blend until smooth.
- Pour into a saucepan and cook over medium-high heat, stirring constantly. Alternatively, you can add to your Instant Pot and cook at high pressure for 1 minute.
- Stir in the lime juice to the sauce.
- Drizzle the sauce over the corn.
- Serve and enjoy!

Nutrition information per serving:
- Calories: 190
- Fat: 4.6g
- Carbohydrates: 33.6g
- Dietary Fiber: 4.7g
- Protein: 9.3g

14. Great Tasting Sweet Potatoes

Time: 30 minutes
Servings: 4
Freestyle SmartPoints: 5
Ingredients:
- 4 raw sweet potatoes
- 2 cups of water

Instructions:
- Rinse and scrub the sweet potatoes
- Add 2 cups of water and a trivet to your Instant Pot.
- Place the potatoes on top of the trivet.
- Lock the lid and cook at high pressure for 18 minutes.
- When the cooking is done, naturally release the pressure.
- Carefully remove the lid and set the potatoes aside.
- Serve and enjoy!

Nutrition information per serving:
- Calories: 57
- Fat: 1g
- Carbohydrates: 15g
- Dietary Fiber: 2g
- Protein: 1g

15. To-Die-For Brussel Sprouts with Shallots

Time: 15 minutes
Servings: 8
Freestyle SmartPoints: 3
Ingredients:
- 2 pounds of Brussel sprouts, trimmed
- 1 or 2 shallots, finely chopped
- 1 tablespoon of olive oil
- ¼ cup of orange juice
- 2 tablespoons of maple syrup
- 1 teaspoon of salt
- 1 teaspoon of black pepper

Instructions:
- Press "Saute" function on your Instant Pot and add the olive oil.
- Once the oil is hot and ready, add the shallots and cook until brown and crispy, stirring occasionally.

- Turn off "Saute" function on your Instant Pot.
- Add the Brussel sprouts, orange juice, maple syrup, salt, and pepper in your Instant Pot.
- Lock the lid and cook at high pressure for 4 minutes.
- When the cooking is done, quick release the pressure and remove the lid.
- Stir until the Brussel sprouts are covered with the shallots and sauce.
- Serve and enjoy!

Nutrition information per serving:

- Calories: 65
- Fat: 2g
- Carbohydrates: 12g
- Dietary Fiber: 3g
- Protein: 3g

Rice and Grains Recipes

1. Incredible Wild Mushroom Rice Risotto

Time: 30 minutes

Servings: 6

Freestyle SmartPoints: 8

Ingredients:
- 4 tablespoons of olive oil
- 4 tablespoons of unsalted butter
- 1 onion, chopped
- 3 garlic cloves, minced
- 1 cup of portabella mushrooms, sliced
- 1 ½ cups of risotto rice
- 4 cups of chicken broth
- 1 ½ cup of Parmigiano-Reggiano cheese

Instructions:
- Press "saute" function on your Instant Pot and add 4 tablespoons of olive oil and 2 tablespoons of butter.
- Once the hot and ready, add the onions and garlic and cook until translucent.
- Add the portabella mushrooms and rice. Stir until the rice is coated with the olive oil.
- Add the chicken broth.
- Lock the lid and cook at high pressure for 7 minutes.
- When the cooking is done, quick release the remaining pressure and stir in the 2 tablespoons of butter.
- Stir in the cheese to the risotto. Serve and enjoy!

Nutrition information per serving:
- Calories: 418
- Fat: 23.2g
- Carbohydrates: 40.8g
- Dietary Fiber: 1.1g
- Protein: 12.1g

2. Fantastic Beef Rice Pilaf

Time: 50 minutes

Servings: 8

Freestyle SmartPoints: 4

Ingredients:
- 2 ½ cups of brown rice, rinsed and drained
- 1 pound of beef chuck stew meat, cut into ¾-inch pieces
- 4 tablespoons of avocado oil
- 4 tablespoons of butter
- 1 large onion, chopped
- 3 large carrots, julienned
- 3 cups of water or beef stock
- 1 tablespoon of salt
- ½ teaspoon of black pepper
- ½ teaspoon of ground paprika
- ½ teaspoon of ground coriander
- 1 whole garlic, unpeeled and cut in half crosswise

Instructions:
- Press "Saute" function on your Instant Pot and add 4 tablespoons of avocado oil.
- Once the oil is hot and ready, add the beef and cook until lightly brown, stirring occasionally.
- Add 4 tablespoons of butter and the chopped onions. Cook for 3 minutes or until softened.
- Add the julienned carrots, salt, black pepper, cumin, paprika, and coriander. Cook for 5 minutes or until softened, stirring occasionally.
- Add the rice, garlic, and water to your Instant Pot.
- Lock the lid and cook at high pressure for 30 minutes.
- When the cooking is done, naturally release the pressure for 10 minutes and quick release the remaining pressure.
- Remove the garlic and set aside.
- Stir everything with a spoon until the ingredients are well incorporated. Adjust the seasoning as needed.
- Serve and enjoy!

Nutrition information per serving:
- Calories: 502
- Fat: 19g
- Carbohydrates: 60g
- Dietary Fiber: 3g
- Protein: 21g

3. Awesome Fried Rice

Time: 11 minutes

Servings: 4

Freestyle SmartPoints: 3

Ingredients:
- 2 cups of long grain rice

- 2 ½ cups of vegetable broth
- 2 carrots, diced
- 3 tablespoons of olive oil
- ½ cup of frozen peas
- 2 medium eggs
- 1 teaspoon of salt
- 1 teaspoon of black pepper

Instructions:
- Add the rice and vegetable broth to your Instant Pot.
- Stir in the carrots.
- Lock the lid and cook at high pressure for 3 minutes.
- When the cooking is done, naturally release the pressure for 10 minutes and quick release the remaining pressure.
- Remove the lid and mix the rice.
- Press "Saute" function and add the olive oil and frozen peas. Cook for 1 minute, stirring occasionally.
- In a small bowl, beat the eggs.
- Make an opening in the middle of the rice and add the eggs.
- Stir the egg into the rice and cook everything for 1 to 2 minutes, stirring frequently.
- Turn off "Saute" function and season with salt and pepper.
- Serve and enjoy!

Nutrition information per serving:
- Calories: 495
- Fat: 13g
- Carbohydrates: 81g
- Dietary Fiber: 2g
- Protein: 10g

4. Welcoming Shrimp Rice

Time: 5 minutes
Servings: 4
Freestyle SmartPoints: 2
Ingredients:
- 1 pound of wild caught shrimps, shell and tail on
- 1 cup of jasmine rice
- 1 ½ cups of chicken broth
- 4 garlic cloves, minced
- ¼ cup of butter
- ¼ cup of parsley, chopped
- 1 teaspoon of salt
- ¼ teaspoon of black pepper
- 1 pinch of crushed red pepper
- 1 medium lemon, juiced

Instructions:
- Add all the ingredients in your Instant Pot except for the parsley and lemon. Place the shrimps on top.
- Lock the lid and cook at high pressure for 5 minutes.
- When the cooking is done, quick release the pressure and remove the lid.
- Remove the shrimp and peel. Return back to your Instant Pot.
- Garnish with parsley and squeeze of lemon juice.
- Serve and enjoy!

Nutrition information per serving:
- Calories: 424
- Fat: 14.3g
- Carbohydrates: 40g
- Dietary Fiber: 0.7g
- Protein: 31.3g

5. Korean Beef and Brown Rice

Time: 32 minutes
Servings: 8
Freestyle SmartPoints: 4
Rice Ingredients:
- 1 ½ cup of brown rice
- 2 cups of water
- ½ teaspoon of salt

Beef Ingredients:
- 1 pound of lean ground beef
- ¼ cup of brown sugar
- ¼ cup of low sodium soy sauce
- 1 tablespoon of sesame oil
- 1 teaspoon of garlic powder
- ¼ teaspoon of ground red pepper
- 2 teaspoons of ginger, minced
- 1 tablespoon of tomato paste

Instructions:
- Grease your Instant Pot with nonstick cooking spray.
- Add the rice, water, and salt to your Instant Pot.

- In an oven-safe dish, add the brown sugar, soy sauce, sesame oil, garlic powder, ground red pepper, ginger, and tomato paste. Mix well.
- Add the ground beef and stir to coat the beef with the sauce mixture.
- Add a trivet to your Instant Pot and place the oven-safe dish on top.
- Lock the lid and cook at high pressure for 22 minutes.
- When the cooking is done, naturally release the pressure for 10 minutes and quick release any remaining pressure.
- Remove the lid and carefully remove the trivet and dish out of your Instant Pot.
- Stir and coat the beef again.
- Scoop rice onto serving plates and top with the beef and juice.
- Serve and enjoy!

Nutrition information per serving:
- Calories: 271
- Fat: 6.2g
- Carbohydrates: 32.2g
- Dietary Fiber: 1.3g
- Protein: 20.4g

6. Lebanese Hashweh Ground Beef and Rice

Time: 30 minutes

Servings: 6

Freestyle SmartPoints: 5

Ingredients:
- 2 tablespoons of olive oil
- ¼ cup of pine nuts
- 1 cup of onions, sliced
- 1 tablespoon of garlic, minced
- 1 pound of ground beef
- ¼ teaspoon of ground cardamom
- 1 ½ teaspoon of ground allspice
- 1 teaspoon of ground cinnamon
- ¼ teaspoon of ground nutmeg
- 1 cup of basmati rice, rinsed and drained
- 1 teaspoon of salt
- 1 teaspoon of ground black pepper
- 1 cup of water
- ¼ cup of cilantro, chopped

Instructions:
- Press "Sauté" function on your Instant Pot and add the olive oil.
- Once the oil is hot and ready, add the pine nuts and cook for 1 to 2 minutes, stirring frequently.
- Add the minced garlic and onions. Stir well and cook until lightly browned.
- Add the ground beef and cook until brown, breaking up the ground beef with a wooden spoon.
- Add all the spices and stir well.
- Add the rice and 1 cups of water.
- Lock the lid and cook at high pressure for 4 minutes.
- When the cooking is done, naturally release the pressure for 10 minutes and quick release the remaining pressure.
- Fluff the rice with a fork and sprinkle with cilantro.
- Serve and enjoy!

Nutrition information per serving:
- Calories: 341
- Fat: 13.5g
- Carbohydrates: 27.7g
- Dietary Fiber: 1.1g
- Protein: 26.2g

7. Tastiest Mexican Black Beans and Rice

Time: 30 minutes

Servings: 4

Freestyle SmartPoints: 4

Ingredients:
- 1 (15-ounce) can of black beans, rinsed and drained
- 1 cup of brown rice
- 1 ½ cup of chicken broth
- ¾ cup of picante sauce
- 1 bay leaf
- 1 teaspoon of cumin
- 1 teaspoon of garlic salt
- 1 lime, juice

Toppings:
- Sour cream
- Tortilla chips
- Grated cheese
- Sliced avocados

Instructions:
- Add the black beans, brown rice, chicken broth, picante sauce, bay leaf, cumin, garlic salt, and lime juice to your Instant Pot.

- Lock the lid and cook at high pressure for 22 minutes.
- When the cooking is done, naturally release the pressure for 10 minutes and quick release the remaining pressure.
- Carefully remove the lid and discard the bay leaf.
- Stir the black beans and rice again and add more sauce as needed.
- Ladle into bowls and top with preferred toppings.
- Serve and enjoy!

Nutrition information per serving:
- Calories: 228
- Fat: 1.2g
- Carbohydrates: 44.4g
- Dietary Fiber: 8g
- Protein: 9.9g

8. Kheema Pulao (Indian Meat and Rice)

Time: 30 minutes
Servings: 6
Freestyle SmartPoints: 4

Pulao Ingredients:
- teaspoons of ghee
- 1 red onion, thinly sliced
- 1 tablespoon of ginger, minced
- 1 tablespoon of garlic, minced
- 1 pound of lean ground beef
- 1 ½ teaspoon of salt
- 1 ½ cup of water
- 1 ½ cup of basmati rice
- 1 cup of frozen peas

Spices Ingredients:
- 1 teaspoon of cumin seeds
- 5 whole cloves
- 5 whole peppercorns
- 1 cinnamon stick, broken into pieces
- 3 teaspoons of garam masala

Instructions:
- Press "Saute" function on your Instant Pot and add the ghee.
- Once the ghee is hot, add the spices and cook for 30 seconds, stirring frequently.
- Add the garlic and ginger and cook for 30 seconds, stirring frequently.
- Add the ground beef and cook until lightly brown, stirring frequently and breaking up all the clumps.
- Add the onions, rice, salt, and water and stir until well combined.
- Lock the lid and cook at high pressure for 4 minutes.
- When the cooking is done, naturally release the pressure for 10 minutes and quick release the remaining pressure.
- Remove the lid and stir in the frozen peas.
- Serve and enjoy!

Nutrition information per serving:
- Calories: 354
- Fat: 6.6g
- Carbohydrates: 43.3g
- Dietary Fiber: 2.4g
- Protein: 27.9g

9. Sensational Chicken and Rice

Time: 25 minutes
Servings: 6
Freestyle SmartPoints: 3

Ingredients:
- 1 pound of boneless, skinless chicken thighs
- 1 tablespoon of avocado oil
- 3 small shallots, chopped
- 3 carrots, chopped
- 1 cup of mushrooms, sliced
- 2 garlic cloves, minced
- 1 ½ cup of white jasmine rice, rinsed and drained
- 1 ½ cup of chicken stock
- 2 tablespoons of fresh thyme leaves, chopped
- 1 teaspoon of salt
- 1 teaspoon of black pepper

Instructions:
- Press "Saute" function on your Instant Pot and add the avocado oil.
- Season the chicken thighs with salt and pepper.
- Once the oil is hot, add the chicken thighs and cook for 5 minutes per side.
- Remove the chicken and set aside.
- Add 1/3 cup of chicken stock to deglaze your Instant Pot. Scrape the bits with a wooden spoon.

- Add the shallots, mushroom, and carrots, and cook for 3 minutes, stirring frequently.
- Add the garlic and cook for 1 minute, stirring frequently.
- Add the chicken stock, rice, thyme and stir until well combined.
- Place the chicken thighs on top of the mixture.
- Lock the lid and cook at high pressure for 10 minutes.
- When the cooking is done, naturally release the pressure and remove the lid.
- Remove the chicken and shred using 2 forks.
- Return the chicken to your Instant Pot and stir.
- Serve and enjoy!

Nutrition information per serving:
- Calories: 347
- Fat: 6.5g
- Carbohydrates: 43.8g
- Dietary Fiber: 1.9g
- Protein: 26.5g

10. Scrumptious Mexican Rice

Time: 18 minutes
Servings: 12
Freestyle SmartPoints: 4
Ingredients:
- 2 tablespoons of avocado oil
- ¼ cup of onions, chopped
- 4 garlic cloves, minced
- 2 cusp of white rice
- 1 teaspoon of salt
- ¾ cups of crushed tomatoes
- 2 ½ cups of chicken stock
- ½ teaspoon of cumin
- ½ teaspoon of garlic powder
- ½ teaspoon of smoked paprika
- ¼ cup of cilantro, chopped

Instructions:
- Press "Saute" function on your Instant Pot and add the avocado oil.
- Once the oil is hot, add the onions and garlic. Cook for 3 minutes or until browned, stirring occasionally.
- Add the white rice and stir the rice until well coated with the oil, garlic, and onions.
- Add the chicken stock, crushed tomatoes, cilantro, cumin, smoked paprika, garlic powder, and salt.
- Lock the lid and cook at high pressure for 8 minutes.
- When the cooking is done, naturally release the pressure for 5 minutes and quick release the remaining pressure.
- Remove the lid. Take a fork and lightly fluff the rice through.
- Serve and enjoy!

Nutrition information per serving:
- Calories: 510
- Fat: 14.2g
- Carbohydrates: 80.3g
- Dietary Fiber: 2.9g
- Protein: 13.6g

Soups, Stews, and Broths Recipes

1. Worldwide Vegetable Soup

Time: 25 minutes

Servings: 6

Freestyle SmartPoints: 1

Ingredients:
- 1 tablespoon of olive oil
- 5 garlic cloves, minced
- 1 onion, chopped
- 2 cups of cauliflower florets
- 5 mushrooms, sliced
- 2 celery stalks, chopped
- 2 carrots, chopped
- 1 ½ cups of zucchini, chopped
- 3 cups of cabbage, chopped
- 1 (15-ounce) can of red kidney beans, drained and rinsed
- 1 (15-ounce) can of diced tomatoes
- 4 cups of vegetable stock
- 1 bay leaf
- 1 teaspoon of Italian seasoning
- 1 teaspoon of paprika
- 1 teaspoon of black pepper
- 1 teaspoon of salt
- 1 tablespoon of lemon juice
- ¼ teaspoon of cayenne pepper
- ½ teaspoon of turmeric

Instructions:
- Press "saute" function on your Instant Pot.
- Add the olive oil, garlic, and onions in your Instant Pot.
- Cook until the onions have softened, stirring occasionally.
- Add the mushrooms and saute for 2 minutes or until fragrant.
- Turn off "saute" function.
- Add the remaining ingredients to your Instant Pot.
- Lock the lid and cook at high pressure for 12 minutes.
- When the cooking is done, naturally release the pressure for 5 minutes and quick release any remaining pressure. Carefully remove the lid.
- Stir the soup again and adjust the seasoning if needed. Serve and enjoy!

Nutrition information per serving:
- Calories: 323
- Fat: 3.8g
- Carbohydrates: 56.6g
- Dietary Fiber: 14.8g
- Protein: 19.5g

2. Hearty Vegetable and Brown Rice Soup

Time: 50 minutes

Servings: 10

Freestyle SmartPoints: 5

Ingredients:
- 1 large onion, chopped
- 3 garlic cloves, minced
- 1 tablespoon of olive oil
- 1 pound of potatoes, chopped
- 3 medium carrots, chopped
- 2 ½ cups of French green beans, trimmed and cut into 2-inch pieces
- 4 celery sticks, chopped
- 1 cup of dry brown rice
- 2 tablespoons of tomato paste
- 1 tablespoon of dried parsley
- 1 tablespoon of dried basil
- 1 teaspoon of dried rosemary
- 1 teaspoon of dried thyme
- 4 cups of vegetable broth
- 2 cups of water
- 2-inch fresh ginger, minced
- 1 teaspoon of salt
- 1 teaspoon of black pepper

Instructions:
- Press "Saute" on your Instant Pot and add the olive oil.
- Once the oil is hot and ready, add the onions and cook for 4 to 5 minutes or until soft and brown.
- Add the garlic and ginger and cook for 1 minute.
- Turn off "Saute" function on your Instant Pot.
- Add the remaining ingredients in your Instant Pot.
- Lock the lid and cook at high pressure for 20 minutes.

- When the cooking is done, naturally release the pressure for 10 minutes and quick release the remaining pressure.
- Remove the lid and stir. Adjust the seasoning as needed.
- Serve and enjoy!

Nutrition information per serving:
- Calories: 160
- Fat: 2.7g
- Carbohydrates: 29.3g
- Dietary Fiber: 4g
- Protein: 5.4g

3. Beyond This World Tomato Soup

Time: 20 minutes

Servings: 8

Freestyle SmartPoints: 2

Ingredients:
- 1 tablespoon of olive oil
- 2 tablespoons of butter
- 1 onion, chopped
- 4 garlic cloves, minced
- 3 (15-ounce) cans of diced tomatoes, undrained
- 4 cups of vegetable broth
- 1 teaspoon of salt
- ½ teaspoon of black pepper
- 1 tablespoon of fresh basil, chopped
- 1 teaspoon of Italian seasoning
- ½ cup of heavy cream
- ½ cup of grated parmesan cheese

Instructions:
- Press "Saute" function on your Instant Pot and add the olive oil and butter.
- Once hot and ready, add the onions and cook for 7 minutes or until translucent.
- Add the garlic and cook for 1 minute, stirring constantly.
- Add the tomatoes, broth, salt, pepper, basil, and Italian seasoning. Stir until well combined.
- Lock the lid and cook at high pressure for 5 minutes.
- When the cooking is done, naturally release the pressure for 15 minutes and quick release the remaining pressure.
- Remove the lid and stir the soup. Adjust the seasoning as needed.
- Use an immersion blender to puree the soup until smooth.
- Stir in the parmesan cheese and heavy cream.
- Serve and enjoy!

Nutrition information per serving:
- Calories: 153
- Fat: 11g
- Carbohydrates: 9.1g
- Dietary Fiber: 2.2g
- Protein: 6.7g

4. Creamy Tortellini, Spinach, and Chicken Soup

Time: 30 minutes

Servings: 8

Freestyle SmartPoints: 3

Ingredients:
- 1 tablespoon of olive oil
- 1 medium onion, chopped
- 2 garlic cloves, minced
- 1 tablespoon of dried basil
- 2 tablespoons of tomato paste
- 4 cups of chicken broth
- 2 (14.5-ounce) cans of diced tomatoes, with juices
- 1 ½ pounds of boneless, skinless chicken breasts, chopped into 1-inch pieces
- 4 cups of frozen or fresh cheese tortellini
- ½ cup of parmesan cheese
- 3 cups of spinach
- 1 cup of coconut cream
- 1 teaspoon of salt
- 1 teaspoon of black pepper

Instructions:
- Press "Saute" function on your Instant Pot and add the olive oil.
- Once the oil is hot and ready, add the onions and cook until translucent, stirring frequently.
- Add the basil, tomatoes, chicken broth, tomatoes, chicken, salt, and pepper. Stir until well combined.
- Lock the lid and cook at high pressure for 15 minutes.
- When the cooking is done, quick release the pressure and remove the lid.
- Stir in the tortellini, spinach, parmesan cheese, and coconut cream.
- Press "Saute" function to heat the tortellini quickly.

- Ladle the soup into serving bowls.
- Serve and enjoy!

Nutrition information per serving:
- Calories: 474
- Fat: 20g
- Carbohydrates: 32.6g
- Dietary Fiber: 4.8g
- Protein: 42g

5. Overpowering Wild Rice Soup

Time: 45 minutes
Servings: 6
Freestyle SmartPoints: 4

Ingredients:
- 5 medium carrots, chopped
- 5 celery stalks, chopped
- ½ onion, chopped
- 3 garlic cloves, minced
- 1 tablespoon of olive oil
- 1 cup of uncooked wild rice
- 8-ounces of fresh mushroom, sliced
- 4 cups of vegetable broth
- 1 teaspoon of salt
- 1 teaspoon of poultry seasoning
- ½ teaspoon of dried thyme

Instructions:
- Press "Saute" on your Instant Pot and add the olive oil.
- Once the oil is hot and ready, add the onions and cook until brown, stirring frequently.
- Add the garlic and cook for 1 minute, stirring frequently.
- Turn off "Saute" function on your Instant Pot.
- Add the remaining ingredients to your Instant Pot.
- Lock the lid and cook at high pressure for 45 minutes.
- When the cooking is done, naturally release or quick release the pressure.
- Remove the lid and stir. Adjust the seasoning as needed. Serve and enjoy!

Nutrition information per serving:
- Calories: 178
- Fat: 3.7g
- Carbohydrates: 28.6g
- Dietary Fiber: 3.7g
- Protein: 9.1g

6. Spicy Sweet Potato Chili

Time: 25 minutes
Servings: 10
Freestyle SmartPoints: 3

Ingredients:
- 1 ½ pound of ground turkey
- 1 pound of sweet potatoes, peeled and chopped
- 1 onion, chopped
- 1 red bell pepper, chopped
- 1 green bell pepper, chopped
- 4 celery stalks, chopped
- 2 tablespoons of olive oil
- 1 (28-ounces) can of diced tomatoes
- 1 (15-ounce) cans of black beans, drained and rinsed
- 4 cups of chicken stock
- 3 tablespoons of minced garlic
- 2 teaspoons of cumin
- 4 chipotle peppers in adobo sauce
- 1 teaspoon of cayenne peppers, minced
- 1 teaspoon of salt
- 1 teaspoon of black pepper

Instructions:
- Press "saute" setting on your Instant Pot and add the ground turkey. Cook until the turkey has browned.
- Add the garlic and onions and cook until softened.
- Add the cumin, cayenne pepper, chipotle peppers, black beans, diced tomatoes, sweet potatoes, and chicken stock. Stir until well combined.
- Lock the lid and cook at high pressure for 10 minutes.
- When the cooking is done, quick release the pressure and remove the lid.
- Press "saute" setting on your Instant Pot and add the bell peppers and celery.
- Allow simmering for 5 minutes or until softened.
- Turn off "saute" setting and adjust the seasoning as needed.
- Serve and enjoy!

Nutrition information per serving:
- Calories: 396
- Fat: 11.5g
- Carbohydrates: 46.8g

- Dietary Fiber: 10.3g
- Protein: 30.4g

7. Lemon Chicken Noodle Soup

Time: 45 minutes

Servings: 10

Freestyle SmartPoints: 4

Ingredients:

- 3 cups of carrots, chopped
- 1 cup of celery, chopped
- 1 cup of green onions, chopped
- 2 garlic cloves, minced
- 2 large chicken breasts, trimmed
- 2 tablespoons of olive oil
- 6 cups of chicken broth
- 2 ½ cups of dry whole wheat egg noodles
- 2 lemons, zested and juiced
- 1 teaspoon of dried thyme
- 1 teaspoon of herbs d' Provence
- ½ cup of parsley, chopped
- 1 teaspoon of salt
- 1 teaspoon of black pepper

Instructions:

- Press "saute" function on your Instant Pot and add 2 tablespoons of olive oil.
- Add the onions, celery, carrots, salt, and black pepper and cook until the carrots have browned.
- Add the garlic and cook for 1 minute, stirring frequently.
- Add the broth and chicken breasts to your Instant Pot.
- Lock the lid and cook at high pressure for 15 minutes.
- When the cooking is done, quick release the pressure and remove the lid.
- Remove the chicken and shred using two forks.
- Add the pasta and close the lid.
- Press "manual" and set for zero minutes. When done, quick release the pressure and remove the lid. Return the shredded chicken.
- Stir in the remaining ingredients.
- Serve and enjoy!

Nutrition information per serving:

- Calories: 180
- Fat: 6.7g
- Carbohydrates: 16.2g
- Dietary Fiber: 2g
- Protein: 13.9g

8. Wonderful Buffalo Chicken Chili

Time: 25 minutes

Servings: 8

Freestyle SmartPoints: 3

Ingredients:

- 1 ½ pounds of ground chicken
- 1 cup of carrots, peeled and sliced
- 1 cup of celery, chopped
- 2 garlic cloves, minced
- 1 small onion, finely chopped
- 1 (28-ounce) can of diced tomatoes
- 1 teaspoon of chili powder
- ¼ cup of hot sauce
- ½ cup of Greek yogurt
- 1/3 cup of blue cheese crumbles

Instructions:

- Press "saute" in your Instant Pot and add the ground chicken. Cook until brown, stirring frequently.
- Add the onions and cook until softened.
- Add the rest of your veggies and stir until well combined.
- In a blender, add the diced tomatoes and blend until slightly smooth. Pour into your Instant Pot.
- Close the lid and cook at high pressure for 15 minutes.
- When the cooking is done, naturally release the pressure for 10 minutes and quick release any remaining pressure. Remove the lid.
- In a small bowl, stir in the blue cheese crumbles and Greek yogurt.
- Ladle the chili into serving bowls and top with Greek yogurt mixture.
- Serve and enjoy!

Nutrition information per serving:

- Calories: 290
- Fat: 10.2g
- Carbohydrates: 11.4g
- Dietary Fiber: 2.1g
- Protein: 37.2g

9. Godly Coconut Curry Butternut Squash Soup

Time: 40 minutes

Servings: 6

Freestyle SmartPoints: 2

Ingredients:
- 4 cups of butternut squash, peeled and cubed
- 3 cups of chicken broth
- 1 cup of carrots, chopped
- 1 onion, chopped
- 1 tablespoon of coconut oil
- 1 cup of coconut milk
- 1 teaspoon of mild curry powder

Instructions:
- Add 1 cup of water and a trivet into your Instant Pot.
- Place the cubed squash pieces and carrots on top of the trivet.
- Close the lid and cook at high pressure for 30 minutes.
- When the cooking is done, quick release the pressure and remove the lid.
- Remove the trivet and discard the water from your Instant Pot. Set the butternut squash and carrots aside.
- Press "saute" function on your Instant Pot and add the coconut oil.
- Once the oil is hot and ready, add the onions and cook until softened, stirring frequently.
- Add the broth, curry powder, carrots, and butternut squash pieces to your Instant Pot and heat through.
- Stir in the coconut milk.
- Use an immersion blender to blend the soup until smooth or reached your desired consistency.
- Serve and enjoy!

Nutrition information per serving:
- Calories: 189
- Fat: 15.2g
- Carbohydrates: 10.5g
- Dietary Fiber: 3.1g
- Protein: 5.5g

10. Famous French Onion Soup

Time: 25 minutes

Servings: 6

Freestyle SmartPoints: 1

Ingredients:
- 2 pounds of yellow onions, peeled and sliced
- 4 tablespoons of butter, unsalted
- 1 tablespoon of brown sugar
- 3 garlic cloves, minced
- 3 tablespoons of flour
- 8 cups of beef broth
- 2 tablespoons of balsamic vinegar
- 1 cup of mozzarella cheese

Instructions:
- Press "saute" setting on your Instant Pot and add the butter.
- Once the butter has melted, add the onions and brown sugar. Cook until onions are golden brown and caramelized, stirring occasionally.
- Stir in the flour and garlic and cook for 1 minute or until the flour is cooked through.
- Add the broth and balsamic vinegar.
- Close and seal the lid of your Instant Pot; cook at high pressure for 5 minutes.
- When the cooking is done, quick release the pressure and remove the lid.
- Preheat your broiler.
- Ladle the soup into 4 to 6 ovenproof serving bowls.
- Top each bowl with mozzarella cheese and broil until the cheese is brown.
- Serve and enjoy!

Nutrition information per serving:
- Calories: 216
- Fat: 10.5g
- Carbohydrates: 20.5g
- Dietary Fiber: 3.4g
- Protein: 10g

11. Amazing Zuppa Toscana

Time: 30 minutes

Servings: 8

Freestyle SmartPoints: 3

Ingredients:
- 2 teaspoons of olive oil
- 1 ½ pounds of ground chicken or ground sausage
- 1 small onion, finely chopped
- 3 garlic cloves, minced
- 3 cups of baby potatoes, chopped
- 1 red bell pepper, chopped
- 4 cups of chicken stock
- 3 cups of kale, stemmed and chopped
- 2/3 cup of low-fat coconut cream
- 1 teaspoon of salt

- 1 teaspoon of black pepper

Instructions:
- Press "saute" function on your Instant Pot and add the olive oil.
- Once the oil is hot and ready, add the onions and cook until softened.
- Add the ground chicken or sausage and cook until brown.
- Add the garlic and cook for 1 minute or until fragrant.
- Add the red bell peppers, potatoes, and chicken stock.
- Close and seal the lid; cook at high pressure for 10 minutes.
- When the cooking is done, quick release the pressure and remove the lid.
- Stir in the kale and coconut cream.
- Press "saute" function and cook until the kale has wilted. Turn off "saute" function.
- Season with salt and black pepper.
- Serve and enjoy!

Nutrition information per serving:
- Calories: 286
- Fat: 12.6g
- Carbohydrates: 15.7g
- Dietary Fiber: 2.7g
- Protein: 27.5g

12. Lovely Curry Cauliflower and Broccoli Soup

Time: 30 minutes

Servings: 8

Freestyle SmartPoints: 3

Ingredients:
- 1 large cauliflower head, chopped
- 1 large broccoli head, chopped
- 1 red bell pepper, chopped
- 1 green bell pepper, chopped
- 4 sweet potatoes, chopped
- 1 onion, finely chopped
- 2 garlic cloves, minced
- 2 cups of unsweetened coconut milk
- 2 cups of vegetable broth
- 1 tablespoon of coconut oil
- 2 tablespoons of yellow curry powder
- 1 teaspoon of cumin
- 1 teaspoon of dried thyme
- ½ teaspoon of cayenne pepper
- 1 teaspoon of salt
- 1 teaspoon of black pepper

Instructions:
- Press "saute" setting on your Instant Pot and add the coconut oil.
- Once the oil is hot and ready, add the onions and cook until translucent, stirring frequently.
- Add the garlic and cook for 1 minute or until fragrant.
- Add the cauliflower, broccoli, and red bell pepper. Cook for an additional minute, stirring occasionally.
- Add the remaining ingredients except for the coconut milk in your Instant Pot.
- Close the lid and cook at high pressure for 3 minutes.
- When the cooking is done, quick release the pressure and remove the lid.
- Stir in the coconut milk and adjust the seasoning as needed.
- Serve and enjoy!

Nutrition information per serving:
- Calories: 264
- Fat: 16.7g
- Carbohydrates: 26.4g
- Dietary Fiber: 7.2g
- Protein: 6.5g

13. Flavorful Chicken Tortilla-Less Soup

Time: 30 minutes

Servings: 8

Freestyle SmartPoints: 2

Ingredients:
- 1 ½ pounds of boneless, skinless chicken breasts
- 2 (10-ounce) cans of diced tomatoes and green chilies
- 1 (14.5-ounce) cans of chicken broth
- 2 zucchinis, chopped
- 1 ¾ cups of low-fat coconut cream
- 2 chipotle peppers in adobo sauce
- 2 teaspoons of adobo sauce
- 1 medium onion, chopped
- 2 teaspoons of garlic powder
- 1 teaspoon of onion powder
- 1 teaspoon of cumin
- 2 teaspoon of chili powder

- 1 teaspoon of dried oregano
- 1 teaspoon of smoked paprika
- 1 teaspoon of salt

Instructions:
- Add all the ingredients except for the coconut cream into your Instant Pot.
- Close and seal the lid.
- Cook at high pressure for 20 minutes.
- When the cooking is done, naturally release the pressure for 10 minutes and quick release any remaining pressure.
- Remove the chicken and chop into pieces.
- Return the cubed chicken to your Instant Pot and stir in the coconut cream.
- Serve and enjoy!

Nutrition information per serving:
- Calories: 169
- Fat: 3.1g
- Carbohydrates: 7.4g
- Dietary Fiber: 1.9g
- Protein: 27.3g

14. Curried Carrot Red Lentil Soup

Time: 35 minutes
Servings: 4
Freestyle SmartPoints: 3

Ingredients:
- 2 teaspoons of olive oil
- 1 cup of onions, chopped
- 1 tablespoon of ginger, grated
- 1 tablespoon of curry powder
- 2 cups of baby carrots, peeled and diced
- 4 cups of vegetable broth
- ¾ cups of dried red lentils rinsed well
- 1 teaspoons of salt
- ¼ teaspoon of ground black pepper

Instructions:
- Press "saute" function on your Instant Pot and add the olive oil.
- Once the oil is hot and ready, add the onions and cook until translucent, stirring frequently.
- Add the ginger and curry powder and cook for 30 seconds, stirring frequently.
- Add the carrots, vegetable broth, red lentils, salt, and black pepper. Stir until well combined.
- Lock the lid and cook at high pressure for 10 minutes.
- When the cooking is done, quick release the pressure and remove the lid.
- Use an immersion blender to puree the soup until smooth.
- Adjust the seasoning as needed.
- Serve and enjoy!

Nutrition information per serving:
- Calories: 209
- Fat: 4.4g
- Carbohydrates: 27.7g
- Dietary Fiber: 12.5g
- Protein: 14.8g

15. Scrumptious Sausage Italian Lentil and Barley Soup

Time: 25 minutes
Servings: 12
Freestyle SmartPoints: 2

Ingredients:
- 2 tablespoons of olive oil
- 1 pound of Italian sausage
- 1 ½ cup of dry lentils, rinsed
- 1 cup of kale, stemmed and finely chopped
- 1/3 cup of pearl barley
- 4 carrots, peeled and chopped
- 1 tablespoon of tomato paste
- 2 celery stalks, chopped
- 1 cup of onions, chopped
- 2 garlic cloves, minced
- 1 tablespoon of Italian seasoning
- ¼ teaspoon of red pepper flakes
- 1 teaspoon of salt
- 1 teaspoon of black pepper
- 5 cups of chicken stock
- 2 (15-ounce) can of crushed tomatoes
- ¼ cup of parsley, chopped
- 2 tablespoons of cider vinegar

Instructions:
- Press "saute" function on your Instant Pot and add the olive oil.
- Once the oil is hot and ready, add the Italian sausage and cook until no longer pink, breaking into smaller pieces with a spoon as you cook.
- Add the onions, celery, and carrots. Cook for 3 to 4 minutes or until the vegetables has softened.
- Stir in the garlic, tomato paste, Italian seasoning, parsley, red pepper flakes, and salt.

- Add the diced tomatoes, cider vinegar, pearl barley, beef stock, and lentils. Stir until well combined.
- Close the lid and cook at high pressure for 10 minutes.
- When the cooking is done, naturally release the pressure for 10 minutes and quick release any remaining pressure.
- Remove the lid and stir in the kale. Serve and enjoy!

Nutrition information per serving:
- Calories: 303
- Fat: 13.6g
- Carbohydrates: 28.8g
- Dietary Fiber: 11.4g
- Protein: 16.7g

16. Delectable Curry Pumpkin

Time: 20 minutes

Servings: 6

Freestyle SmartPoints: 4

Ingredients:
- 1 onion, chopped
- 2 teaspoons of olive oil
- 2 tablespoons of butter
- 3 tablespoons of all-purpose flour
- 2 tablespoons of curry powder
- 5 cups of vegetable broth
- 4 cups of pumpkin puree
- 1 ½ cups of low-fat coconut cream
- 2 tablespoons of soy sauce
- ½ tablespoon of brown sugar
- 1 teaspoon of lemon juice
- ½ teaspoon of lemon zest
- ¼ teaspoon of cayenne pepper
- ½ teaspoon of salt
- ½ teaspoon of black pepper

Instructions:
- Press "saute" function on your Instant Pot and add the olive oil.
- When the oil is hot and ready, add the onions and cook until softened.
- Remove and set aside.
- Melt the butter in your Instant Pot and stir in the flour and curry powder until smooth.
- Continue to stir until the mixture begins to bubble.
- Gradually stir in the vegetable broth.
- Add the pumpkin, onions, soy sauce, brown sugar, salt, and black pepper into your Instant Pot.
- Close the lid and cook at high pressure for 3 minutes.
- When the cooking is done, quick release the pressure and remove the lid.
- Stir in the coconut cream.
- Use an immersion blender and blend until smooth.
- Stir in the lemon juice and lemon zest. Serve and enjoy!

Nutrition information per serving:
- Calories: 307
- Fat: 21.7g
- Carbohydrates: 24.4g
- Dietary Fiber: 7.3g
- Protein: 8.5g

17. Hearty Golden Lentil and Spinach Soup

Time: 35 minutes

Servings: 4

Freestyle SmartPoints:

Ingredients:
- 2 teaspoons of olive oil
- 1 cup of onions, chopped
- 1 cup of carrots, chopped
- ½ cup of celery, chopped
- 4 garlic cloves, minced
- 2 teaspoons of ground cumin
- 1 teaspoon of ground turmeric
- 1 teaspoon of dried thyme
- 1 teaspoon of salt
- ¼ teaspoon of black pepper
- 1 cup of dry brown lentils, rinsed
- 4 cups of vegetable broth
- 6 cups of baby spinach

Instructions:
- Press "saute" function on your Instant Pot and add the olive oil.
- When the oil is hot and ready, add the onions, carrots, and celery. Cook until tender, stirring occasionally.
- Add the garlic, cumin, turmeric, thyme, salt, and black pepper. Cook for 1 minute, stirring constantly.
- Add the lentils and pour in the vegetable broth. Stir until well combined.

- Lock the lid on your Instant Pot and cook at high pressure for 12 minutes.
- When the cooking is done, quick release the pressure and remove the lid.
- Stir in the spinach until wilted.
- Serve and enjoy!

Nutrition information per serving:
- Calories: 98
- Fat: 4g
- Carbohydrates: 9.3g
- Dietary Fiber: 2.6g
- Protein: 7g

18. Delicious Italian Farmhouse Vegetable Soup

Time: 25 minutes

Servings: 4

Freestyle SmartPoints: 0

Ingredients:
- 1 tablespoon of olive oil
- 1 onion, chopped
- 2 celery sticks, sliced
- 2 carrots, peeled and sliced
- 6 mushrooms, sliced
- 4 porcini mushrooms, sliced
- 4 garlic cloves, minced
- ½ long red chili, sliced
- 2 cups of kale, stemmed and chopped
- 1 zucchini, chopped
- 1 cup of tomatoes, chopped
- 4 cups of vegetable stock
- 1 tablespoon of lemon juice
- 1 teaspoon of lemon zest
- 1 teaspoon of salt
- 1 teaspoon of black pepper

Instructions:
- Press "saute" function on your Instant Pot and add the olive oil.
- Once the oil is hot and ready, add the onion, salt, celery, and carrots. Cook for 2 minutes, stirring occasionally.
- Add the mushrooms, chili, and garlic. Cook for 1 minute, stirring occasionally.
- Add the remaining ingredients and stir until well combined.
- Lock the lid and cook at high pressure for 10 minutes.
- When the cooking is done, naturally release the pressure for 10 minutes and quick release any remaining pressure. Carefully remove the lid.
- Serve and enjoy!

Nutrition information per serving:
- Calories: 106
- Fat: 4.4g
- Carbohydrates: 15.1g
- Dietary Fiber: 3.3g
- Protein: 4.1g

19. Creamy Cauliflower Soup

Time: 30 minutes

Servings: 5

Freestyle SmartPoints: 2

Ingredients:
- 2 tablespoons of olive oil
- 1 onion, chopped
- 2 garlic cloves, minced
- 2 carrots, shredded
- 1 large head of cauliflower, chopped
- 1 cup of coconut cream
- 2/3 cup of mozzarella cheese, grated
- 1/3 cup of parmesan cheese, grated
- 2 cups of vegetable broth
- ¼ cup of butter
- ¼ cup of all-purpose flour
- 1 tablespoon of parsley
- 1 teaspoon of salt
- 1 teaspoon of black pepper

Instructions:
- Press "saute" setting on your Instant Pot and add the butter.
- Once the butter has melted, add the onions and cook until tender and golden.
- Add the garlic and cook for 1 minute.
- Add the carrots, cauliflower, vegetable broth, salt, and black pepper.
- Close the lid and cook at high pressure for 5 minutes.
- When the cooking is done, naturally release the pressure for 5 minutes and quick release any remaining pressure.
- Remove the lid from your Instant Pot.
- In a saucepan over medium-high heat, melt ¼ cup of butter.

- Stir in the ¼ cup of flour and stir until the mixture thickens and turns golden brown.
- Add the mozzarella cheese, parmesan cheese, and coconut cream in your Instant Pot and stir until melted.
- Add the flour mixture to the soup and stir until thickened.
- Garnish with parsley and adjust the seasoning as needed. Serve and enjoy!

Nutrition information per serving:
- Calories: 405
- Fat: 31.3g
- Carbohydrates: 22.3g
- Dietary Fiber: 6.6g
- Protein: 14.1g

20. Supreme Taco Soup

Time: 30 minutes
Servings: 10
Freestyle SmartPoints: 0

Ingredients:
- 1 ½ pound of ground turkey breast
- 1 large onion, chopped
- 1 tablespoon of olive oil
- 2 tablespoons of package Hidden Valley ranch dressing
- 2 tablespoons of taco seasoning mix
- 4 cups of chicken broth
- 1 (15-ounce) can of pinto beans
- 1 (15-ounce) can of hot chili beans
- 1 (15-ounce) can of whole kernel corns
- 1 (15-ounce) can of stewed tomatoes, Mexican flavor
- 1 (15-ounce) can of stewed tomatoes, any flavor
- 1 teaspoon of garlic powder
- 1 teaspoon of salt
- 1 teaspoon of black pepper

Instructions:
- Press "saute" function on your Instant Pot and add the ground turkey.
- Cook until the turkey is browned, stirring frequently.
- Add the olive oil and onions and cook for 5 minutes or until onions have softened.
- Add the remaining ingredients to your Instant Pot.
- Lock the lid and cook at high pressure for 15 minutes.
- When the cooking is done, quick release the pressure and remove the lid.
- Stir the soup again and adjust the seasoning as needed.
- Serve and enjoy!

Nutrition information per serving:
- Calories: 249
- Fat: 3g
- Carbohydrates: 39g
- Dietary Fiber: 8g
- Protein: 19g

21. Yummy Tomato Spinach Soup

Time: 20 minutes
Servings: 6
Freestyle SmartPoints: 1

Ingredients:
- 1 onion, chopped
- 2 garlic cloves, minced
- 2 carrots, grated
- 2 tablespoons of olive oil
- 1 pound of fresh spinach
- 1 (28-ounce) can of crushed tomatoes
- 1 ½ cups of chicken broth
- 2 teaspoons of dried basil
- 1 teaspoon of salt
- 1 teaspoon of black pepper
- 1 (5-ounce) can of evaporated milk

Instructions:
- Press "saute" setting on your Instant Pot and add the olive oil.
- Once the oil is hot, add the onions and carrots and cook until softened, stirring occasionally.
- Add the garlic and cook for 1 minute or until fragrant.
- Add the remaining ingredients except for the spinach and evaporated milk.
- Lock the lid and cook at high pressure for 15 minutes.
- When the cooking is done, naturally release the pressure for 10 minutes and quick release any remaining pressure.
- Remove the lid and carefully stir in the evaporated milk and spinach.
- Serve and enjoy!

Nutrition information per serving:
- Calories: 169

- Fat: 7.1g
- Carbohydrates: 20g
- Dietary Fiber: 6.8g
- Protein: 8.6g

22. Flavorsome Chunky Beef, Cabbage, and Tomato Soup

Time: 30 minutes

Servings: 7

Freestyle SmartPoints: 3

Ingredients:
- 1 pound of ground beef
- 1 onion, chopped
- 2 celery stalks, chopped
- 2 carrots, chopped
- 1 (28-ounce) can of diced tomatoes
- 5 cups of green cabbage, chopped
- 4 cups of beef stock
- 2 bay leaves
- 1 teaspoon of garlic powder
- 1 teaspoon of salt
- 1 teaspoon of black pepper

Instructions:
- Press "saute" function on your Instant Pot and add the olive oil.
- When the oil is hot, add the ground beef and cook until brown.
- When the ground beef has browned, add the onions, celery, and carrots and cook for 4 minutes or until softened.
- Add the tomatoes, cabbage, beef stock, and bay leaves.
- Lock the lid and cook at high pressure for 20 minutes.
- When the cooking is done, naturally release the pressure and remove the lid.
- Remove the bay leaves.
- Serve and enjoy!

Nutrition information per serving:
- Calories: 181
- Fat: 6g
- Carbohydrates: 14g
- Dietary Fiber: 2g
- Protein: 15.5g

23. Unique Loaded Baked Potato Soup

Time: 25 minutes

Servings: 6

Freestyle SmartPoints: 7

Ingredients:
- 2 pounds of potatoes
- 5 bacon slices, chopped
- ¼ cup of butter
- ¼ cup of flour
- 4 cups of milk
- ½ cup of sour cream
- ½ cup of cheddar cheese, grated
- 3 green onions, diced
- 1 teaspoon of bouillon chicken base
- 1 teaspoon of salt
- ½ teaspoon of black pepper

Instructions:
- Press "saute" function on your Instant Pot and add the bacon bits.
- Cook the bacon until brown and crispy. Once done, remove the bacon and set aside. Turn off "saute" function.
- Add 1 cup of water and a trivet inside your Instant Pot.
- Place the potatoes on top of the trivet.
- Lock the lid and cook at high pressure for 10 minutes.
- When the cooking is done, quick release the pressure and remove the lid.
- Remove the potatoes and set aside.
- Remove the water and discard the trivet.
- Press "saute" setting on your Instant Pot and add the butter.
- Once the butter has melted, add 1 tablespoon of flour and stir until begins to bubble.
- Add the milk and bouillon and start to whisk.
- Stir in the sour cream, cheddar cheese, diced onions, and bacon.
- Smash the potatoes with a potato masher and stir the potatoes into the soup.
- Add salt and black pepper to the soup. Serve and enjoy!

Nutrition information per serving:
- Calories: 439
- Fat: 25g
- Carbohydrates: 37.5g
- Dietary Fiber: 4g
- Protein: 17.5g

24. Exquisite Broccoli Cheese Soup

Time: 15 minutes
Servings: 6
Freestyle SmartPoints: 2
Ingredients:
- ¼ cup of butter
- 1 onion, finely chopped
- 2 cups of carrots, chopped
- 2 garlic cloves, minced
- ¼ cup of flour
- 3 cups of vegetable stock
- 6 cups of broccoli florets
- 1 teaspoon of paprika
- 1 teaspoon of Dijon mustard
- 1 ½ cups of Monterey jack cheese, shredded
- 1 ½ cups of sharp cheddar cheese, shredded
- ½ cup of milk
- ½ cup of coconut cream
- 1 teaspoon of salt
- 1 teaspoon of black pepper

Instructions:
- Press "saute" setting on your Instant Pot and add the butter.
- When the butter is melted, add the onions and carrots and cook for 3 minutes or until onions are translucent.
- Stir in the garlic and flour and cook for 1 minute.
- Stir in the broth and continue to stir until flour lumps are gone.
- Add the broccoli and vegetable stock to your Instant Pot.
- Lock the lid and cook at high pressure for 8 minutes.
- When the cooking is done, quick release the pressure and remove the lid.
- Stir in the paprika, Dijon mustard, salt, and black pepper until well incorporated.
- Stir in the cheeses until fully melted.
- Once the cheese has melted, add the milk and coconut cream.
- If you prefer, use an immersion blender to blend the soup until reached your desired consistency. Serve and enjoy!

Nutrition information per serving:
- Calories: 228
- Fat: 14.6g
- Carbohydrates: 18.5g
- Dietary Fiber: 5.1g
- Protein: 7.2g

Appetizers and Side Dishes Recipes

1. Candied Pecans

Time: 20 minutes
Servings: 12
Freestyle SmartPoints: 3
Ingredients:
- 4 cups of raw pecans
- 2/3 cup of pure maple syrup
- 1 tablespoon of water
- 1 teaspoon of ground cinnamon
- ½ teaspoon of ground nutmeg
- 1/8 teaspoon of ground ginger
- 1/8 teaspoon of cayenne pepper
- A pinch of salt

Instructions:
- Press "saute" function on your Instant Pot and add all the ingredients inside.
- Saute until the pecans are tender.
- Add ½ cup of water to your Instant Pot.
- Lock the lid and cook at high pressure for 10 minutes.
- When the cooking is done, quick release the pressure and remove the lid.
- Remove the pecans from your Instant Pot and spread on a baking sheet.
- Bake inside your oven at 350 degrees Fahrenheit for 5 minutes. Be careful as they can burn very quickly.
- Serve and enjoy!

Nutrition information per serving:
- Calories: 582
- Fat: 56.1g
- Carbohydrates: 22g
- Dietary Fiber: 7.1g
- Protein: 7.2g

2. Delicious Roasted Onion Garlic Hummus

Time: 2 hours
Servings: 8
Freestyle SmartPoints: 4
Ingredients:
- 1 pound of Garbanzo beans, dried
- 7 cups of water
- 2 teaspoons of water
- 1 onion, chopped
- 5 garlic cloves, minced
- 3 tablespoons of olive oil
- 1 tablespoon of ghee, melted
- ¼ teaspoon of ground cumin
- 2 teaspoons of salt
- ¼ cup of lemon juice
- 1 teaspoon of lemon zest
- 1 ½ tablespoon of pure sesame oil
- 1 cup of natural sesame seeds, toasted
- Paprika (to garnish)

Instructions:
- Press "saute" function on your Instant Pot" and add 2 tablespoons of olive oil.
- Once the oil is hot and ready, add the onions and cook until translucent.
- Add the garlic and cook for 1 minute or until fragrant, stirring frequently.
- Remove the onion and garlic and set aside. Turn off "saute" function.
- Add the garbanzo beans and water to your Instant Pot.
- Lock the lid and cook at high pressure for 1 hour.
- When the cooking is done, quick release the pressure and remove the lid.
- Remove the lid and season with salt.
- Lock the lid and cook at high pressure for 30 minutes.
- When the cooking is done, quick release the pressure and remove the lid.
- Drain the Garbanzo beans and reserve the liquid.
- In a baking sheet, add sesame seeds coated with melted ghee.
- Place in your oven and toast for 375 degrees Fahrenheit for 25 minutes.
- In a food processor, add the toasted sesame seeds, garlic, ½ cup of bean water, and 1 tablespoon of olive oil. Process until smooth.
- Add the lemon, cumin, sesame oil, and garbanzo beans to the food processor and pulse until smooth.
- Add the remaining ingredients and continue to process, leaving just tiny bits of onions and garlic. Sprinkle with paprika. Serve and enjoy!

Nutrition information per serving:
Calories: 406, Fat: 22.7g, Carbohydrates: 40.1g, Dietary Fiber: 12.3g, Protein: 14.3g

3. Great Tasting Broccoli and Cheddar Pasta

Time: 10 minutes

Servings: 4

Freestyle SmartPoints: 8

Ingredients:
- 1 pound of pasta
- 4 cups of water
- 2 cups of cheddar cheese, shredded
- 1 cup of frozen broccoli florets
- 1 cup of milk
- 1 teaspoon of salt
- 1 teaspoon of black pepper

Instructions:
- Add 4 cups of water and pasta to your Instant Pot.
- Add a steamer rack on top of the pasta and place the broccoli on top.
- Lock the lid and cook at high pressure for 4 minutes.
- When the cooking is done, quick release the pressure and remove the lid.
- Remove the steamer rack and set the broccoli aside.
- Stir in the milk and cheddar cheese to the pasta until the cheese is melted.
- Stir in the broccoli and add the salt and black pepper
- Serve and enjoy!

Nutrition information per serving:
- Calories: 964
- Fat: 46g
- Carbohydrates: 90g
- Dietary Fiber: 4g
- Protein: 45g

4. Creamy Macaroni and Cheese

Time: 10 minutes

Servings: 4

Freestyle SmartPoints:

Ingredients:
- 16-ounces of pasta
- 3 tablespoons of butter
- 1 teaspoon of dry mustard
- ½ teaspoon of garlic salt
- ½ teaspoon of salt
- 4 cups of water
- 1 (5-ounce) can of evaporated milk
- 3 cups of shredded extra-sharp cheddar cheese
- 1 cup of shredded Monterey Jack
- ¼ cup of shredded parmesan cheese

Instructions:
- Add the pasta, butter, seasonings, and water into your Instant Pot.
- Lock the lid and cook at high pressure for 4 minutes.
- When the cooking is done, quick release the pressure and remove the lid.
- Stir in the evaporated milk and half of each cheese.
- Add the remaining cheeses and stir until the cheese has melted.
- Adjust the seasoning as needed. Remove the macaroni and cheese and allow the sauce to thicken in your Instant Pot.
- Serve and enjoy!

Nutrition information per serving:
- Calories: 593
- Fat: 22.7g
- Carbohydrates: 67.3g
- Dietary Fiber: 0.6g
- Protein: 29.5g

5. Lovely Meatballs

Time: 20 minutes

Servings: 6

Freestyle SmartPoints: 6

Ingredients:
- 1 ½ pounds of ground lean beef
- ½ cup of onions, grated
- ½ cup of panko breadcrumbs
- ½ cup of parmesan cheese, grated
- 2 eggs, beaten
- 2 garlic cloves, minced
- 2 tablespoons of low-fat milk
- 1 teaspoon of salt
- ½ teaspoon of oregano
- 1/4 teaspoon of black pepper
- 4 cups of marinara sauce

Instructions:
- In a large bowl, add the ground beef, onions, breadcrumbs, parmesan cheese, eggs, garlic, milk, salt, oregano, and black pepper. Use your hands to mix the ingredients together.

- Form the ground beef mixture into small meatballs.
- Grease your Instant Pot with nonstick cooking spray and add the marinara sauce.
- Place the meatballs over the sauce.
- Lock the lid and cook at high pressure for 7 minutes.
- When the cooking is done, naturally release the pressure for 5 minutes and quick release the remaining pressure.
- Remove the lid from your Instant Pot.
- Stir the meatballs again and sprinkle with salt and pepper.
- Serve and enjoy!

Nutrition information per serving:
- Calories: 480
- Fat: 17.6g
- Carbohydrates: 31.7g
- Dietary Fiber: 5g
- Protein: 46.8g

6. Party-Perfect Black Bean Dip

Time: 45 minutes
Servings: 24
Freestyle SmartPoints: 4
Ingredients:
- 1 ½ cup of dried black beans, rinsed
- 1 medium onion, chopped
- 4 garlic cloves, minced
- 2 medium jalapenos, chopped
- 1 (14.5-ounce) can of diced tomatoes
- 1 ¾ cup of vegetable broth
- 1 ½ tablespoon of avocado oil
- 1 lime, juice
- 2 teaspoons of ground cumin
- 1 teaspoon of smoked paprika
- 1 teaspoon of salt
- ½ teaspoon of chili powder
- ½ teaspoon of ground coriander

Instructions:
- Add the black beans to your Instant Pot.
- Add the onions, garlic, jalapenos, tomatoes, vegetable broth, avocado oil, lime juice, and spices to your Instant Pot. Stir until well combined.
- Lock the lid and cook at high pressure for 30 minutes.
- When the cooking is done, naturally release the pressure for 10 minutes and quick release the remaining pressure.
- Use an immersion blender to blend the beans until creamy or reached your desired consistency.
- Serve and enjoy as your favorite topping.

Nutrition information per serving:
- Calories: 51
- Fat: 0.4g
- Carbohydrates: 9.3g
- Dietary Fiber: 2.3g
- Protein: 3g

7. Sweet and Spicy Meatballs

Time: 30 minutes
Servings: 8
Freestyle SmartPoints: 1
Ingredients:
- 1 pound of lean ground beef (or 1 package of cooked meatballs)
- 1 egg, beaten
- 1 onion, chopped
- 1 teaspoon of salt
- 1 teaspoon of black pepper
- 2 tablespoons of coconut oil
- 12-ounces of chili sauce
- 12-ounces of grape jelly
- ½ cup of water
- ½ tablespoon of crushed red pepper
- ½ teaspoon of cayenne pepper

Instructions:
- In a large bowl, add the ground beef, onions, eggs, salt, and pepper. Mix until well combined.
- Shape the ground beef mixture into meatballs.
- Press "Saute" function on your Instant Pot and add the coconut oil.
- Once the oil is hot and ready, add the meatballs and cook until brown on all sides. You may need to work in batches.
- In a bowl, add the chili sauce, grape jelly, water, crushed red pepper, and cayenne pepper. Mix until well combined.
- Pour the sauce over the meatballs and stir until well coated.
- Lock the lid and cook at high pressure for 10 minutes.

- When the cooking is done, quick or naturally release the pressure. Carefully remove the lid.
- Serve and enjoy!

Nutrition information per serving:
- Calories: 271
- Fat: 7.7g
- Carbohydrates: 31.3g
- Dietary Fiber: 0.9g
- Protein: 18.4g

8. Enjoyable Pizza Dip

Time: 35 minutes
Servings: 8
Freestyle SmartPoints: 3
Ingredients:
- 1 (8-ounce) block of cream cheese, softened
- ½ cup of spaghetti sauce or pizza sauce
- 1 cup of shredded mozzarella cheese
- ½ teaspoon of dried basil
- ½ teaspoon of salt

Instructions:
- Grease an oven safe dish that will fit in your Instant Pot with nonstick cooking spray.
- Spread the cream cheese onto the dish.
- Pour the spaghetti sauce over the cream cheese and sprinkle with mozzarella cheese.
- Sprinkle with dried basil and salt.
- Add 2 cups of water and a trivet to your Instant Pot.
- Place the oven safe dish on top of the trivet.
- Lock the lid and cook at high pressure for 20 minutes.
- When the cooking is done, quick release the pressure and remove the lid.
- Remove the dish and allow to cool before serving.
- Serve and enjoy!

Nutrition information per serving:
- Calories: 121
- Fat: 8g
- Carbohydrates: 3g
- Dietary Fiber: 0g
- Protein: 7g

9. Artichoke and Spinach Dip

Time: 6 minutes
Servings: 10
Freestyle SmartPoints: 3
Ingredients:
- 8-ounces of cream cheese
- 1 pound of frozen spinach
- 16-ounces of shredded parmesan cheese
- 1 cup of shredded mozzarella cheese
- ½ cup of chicken broth
- 1 (14-ounce) can of artichoke hearts, drained
- ½ cup of low-fat sour cream
- ½ cup of low-fat mayonnaise
- 3 garlic cloves, crushed
- 1 teaspoon of onion powder

Instructions:
- Add the garlic and ½ cup of chicken broth to your Instant Pot.
- Add the artichokes to your Instant Pot.
- Place the frozen spinach, sour cream, cream cheese, mayonnaise, and onion powder into your Instant Pot.
- Lock the lid and cook at high pressure for 4 minutes.
- When the cooking is done, quick release the pressure and remove the lid.
- Stir in the parmesan cheese and mozzarella cheese.
- Transfer to a serving bowl.
- Serve and enjoy!

Nutrition information per serving:
- Calories: 330
- Fat: 26g
- Carbohydrates: 6g
- Dietary Fiber: 2g
- Protein: 15g

10. Appetizing Tomato Mac and Cheese with Crispy Bacon

Time: 25 minutes
Servings: 12
Freestyle SmartPoints: 9
Ingredients:
- 2 pounds of pasta shells
- 8 slices of bacon, chopped
- 6 cups of water
- ¼ cup of butter
- 2 cups of low-fat milk
- ¼ cup of low-fat sour cream
- 1 (14.5-ounce) can of diced tomatoes, drained

- 2 cups of cheddar cheese, shredded
- 1 cup of weight watchers cottage cheese
- ½ cup of parmesan cheese, shredded
- 1 tablespoon of garlic salt
- 2 teaspoons of black pepper

Instructions:

- Press "saute" function on your Instant Pot. Add the bacon and cook for 8 minutes or until crispy.
- Remove the bacon and set aside.
- Turn "Saute" function off.
- Add the pasta and 6 cups of water to your Instant Pot.
- Lock the lid and cook at high pressure for 4 minutes.
- Carefully remove the lid and stir in the milk, sour cream, diced tomatoes, cheddar cheese, parmesan cheese, cottage cheese, garlic salt and black pepper.
- Press "saute" function and cook for 4 minutes or until the cheese has melted, stirring frequently.
- Stir in the bacon until well combined.
- Serve and enjoy!

Nutrition information per serving:
- Calories: 450
- Fat: 19.4g
- Carbohydrates: 46g
- Dietary Fiber: 0.4g
- Protein: 22.4g

11. Buffalo Hot Wings

Time: 20 minutes
Servings: 6
Freestyle SmartPoints: 4
Ingredients:

- 4 pounds of chicken wings
- ½ cup of Frank's RedHot Cayenne Pepper Sauce
- ½ cup of butter, melted
- 1 tablespoon of Worcestershire sauce
- 1 cup of water
- 1 teaspoon of salt
- ½ teaspoon of black pepper

Instructions:

- In a bowl, add the Frank's RedHot Cayenne Pepper Sauce, butter, Worcestershire sauce, salt, and black pepper. Mix until well combined.
- Add 1 cup of water and a trivet to your Instant Pot.
- Place the chicken wings on top of the trivet.
- Lock the lid and cook at high pressure for 5 minutes.
- When the cooking is done, naturally release the pressure for 5 minutes and quick release the remaining pressure.
- Remove the lid and place the chicken wings on a baking sheet.
- Brush each chicken wing with the hot sauce mixture.
- Place the baking sheet inside your broiler and broil for 5 minutes.
- Remove the baking sheet from your oven and toss the wings with the remaining hot sauce mixture.
- Serve and enjoy!

Nutrition information per serving:
- Calories: 712
- Fat: 37.8g
- Carbohydrates: 0.4g
- Dietary Fiber: 0.1g
- Protein: 87.6g

12. Pleasant Cheddar Bacon Ale Dip

Time: 25 minutes
Servings: 10
Freestyle SmartPoints: 6
Ingredients:

- 18-ounces of cream cheese softened
- ¼ cup of low-fat sour cream
- 1 ½ tablespoon of Dijon mustard
- 1 teaspoon of garlic powder
- 1 cup of beer
- 1 pound of bacon strips, chopped
- 2 cups of shredded cheddar cheese
- ¼ cup of heavy whipping cream

Instructions:

- Press "saute" function on your Instant Pot and add the bacon.
- Cook the bacon until brown and crispy. Once done, remove and set aside. Turn off "saute" function.
- Add cream cheese, sour cream, mustard, and garlic powder inside your Instant Pot. Stir until well combined.
- Stir in the beer and bacon, reserving 2 tablespoons.

- Lock the lid and cook at high pressure for 5 minutes.
- When the cooking is done, quick release the pressure and remove the lid.
- Press "saute" function and stir in the cheese and heavy cream.
- Cook and stir until the mixture has thickened about 3 to 4 minutes.
- Transfer the mixture to a serving dish and sprinkle with reserved bacon bits.
- Serve and enjoy!

Nutrition information per serving:
- Calories: 549
- Fat: 46.6g
- Carbohydrates: 3.6g
- Dietary Fiber: 0.1g
- Protein: 26.7g

13. Cheesy Rotel Queso Dip

Time: 20 minutes

Servings: 11

Freestyle SmartPoints: 2

Ingredients:
- 2 cups of ground Italian sausage
- 1 (10-ounce) can of Rotel tomatoes with chiles, diced and drained
- 2 jalapenos, seeded and diced
- 1 poblano pepper, diced
- 1 cup of onions, minced
- 3 garlic cloves, minced
- 2 teaspoons of canola oil
- ¼ cup of cilantro, chopped
- 2 cups of shredded reduced-fat sharp Cheddar, Sargento
- ½ cup of low sodium chicken broth
- 1 cup of skim milk
- 3 tablespoons of cornstarch
- 1 lime, juice and zest
- ½ teaspoon of ground cumin
- 1 teaspoon of ancho chili powder

Instructions:
- In a small bowl, mix ¼ cup of skim milk with 3 tablespoons of cornstarch. Set aside.
- Press "saute" function on your Instant Pot and add the canola oil.
- Once the oil is hot and ready, add the onions, garlic, poblano, and jalapeno. Cook until softened, about 5 to 7 minutes, stirring frequently.
- Turn off "saute" function on your Instant Pot.
- Add the chicken broth, sausage, tomatoes, and 1 cup of cheese to your Instant Pot.
- Lock the lid and cook at high pressure for 5 minutes.
- When the cooking is done, naturally release the pressure for 5 minutes and quick release the remaining pressure.
- Press "saute" function on your Instant Pot and stir in the remaining ingredients.
- Cook and stir until the cheese has completely melted. Serve and enjoy!

Nutrition information per serving:
- Calories: 92.5
- Fat: 4.6g
- Carbohydrates: 7g
- Dietary Fiber: 1g
- Protein: 6.5g

14. Cabbage with Turkey Sausage

Time: 10 minutes

Servings: 8

Freestyle SmartPoints: 2

Ingredients:
- 1 pound of Turkey sausage, sliced
- 1 large cabbage head, chopped
- 1 onion, chopped
- 3 garlic cloves, minced
- 2 teaspoons of sugar
- 2 teaspoons of balsamic vinegar
- 2 teaspoons of Dijon mustard
- 1 tablespoon of olive oil
- 1 teaspoon of salt
- 1 teaspoon of black pepper

Instructions:
- Press "Saute" function on your Instant Pot and add the olive oil.
- Once the oil is hot and ready, add the Turkey sausage and onions. Cook until slightly browned.
- Add the cabbage and remaining ingredients to your Instant Pot. Cook until the cabbage cooks down, stirring frequently.
- Turn off "Saute" function on your Instant Pot. Adjust the seasoning as needed.
- Serve and enjoy!

Nutrition information per serving:

- Calories: 220
- Fat: 17.9g
- Carbohydrates: 3g
- Dietary Fiber: 0.5g
- Protein: 11.3g

15. Fit for a King Spinach Artichoke Macaroni and Cheese

Time: 25 minutes

Servings: 6

Freestyle SmartPoints: 6

Ingredients:
- 2 tablespoons of olive oil
- 1 large onion, finely chopped
- 10 garlic cloves, minced
- 1 can of artichoke hearts, drained and roughly chopped
- 1 pound of pasta
- 12-ounces of baby spinach
- 6 cups of vegetable broth
- 1 teaspoon of red pepper flakes
- 1 teaspoon of salt
- 1 teaspoon of black pepper
- 4-ounces of cream cheese softened
- ¼ cup of parmesan cheese, grated
- 1 cup of shredded low-fat mozzarella

Instructions:
- Press "saute" function on your Instant Pot and add the olive oil.
- Once the oil is hot and ready, add the onions and cook for 2 minutes or until translucent.
- Add the garlic and cook for 1 minute or until fragrant, stirring frequently.
- Add the artichoke hearts and cook for another minute.
- Add the pasta and 5 cups of vegetable broth.
- Lock the lid and cook at high pressure for 4 minutes.
- When the cooking is done, quick release the pressure and remove the lid.
- Stir in the remaining vegetable broth. If the pasta looks watery, don't add.
- Press "saute" function on your Instant Pot and fold in the baby spinach. Cook until the spinach wilts.
- Stir in the cream cheese, mozzarella, and parmesan.
- Season with red pepper flakes, salt, and black pepper. Stir everything until everything is well combined and the cheese has melted. Serve and enjoy!

Nutrition information per serving:
- Calories: 509
- Fat: 18g
- Carbohydrates: 65g
- Dietary Fiber: 4g
- Protein: 22g

16. Smoky Baked Beans

Time: 45 minutes

Servings: 12

Freestyle SmartPoints: 2

Ingredients:
- 1 pound of dried navy beans, soaked overnight and rinsed
- 1 tablespoon of salt
- 8 slices of bacon, cut into ½-inch pieces
- 1 large onion, chopped
- 2 ½ cups of chicken stock
- ½ cup of molasses
- ½ cup of ketchup
- ¼ cup of packed brown sugar
- 1 teaspoon of dry mustard
- ½ teaspoon of black pepper

Instructions:
- Press "saute" function on your Instant Pot and add the bacon bits. Cook until brown and crispy, stirring occasionally.
- Remove the bacon bits and place on paper towels.
- Add the onions to the bacon grease and cook until tender, about 3 minutes.
- Add the chicken stock, molasses, ketchup, brown sugar, dry mustard, salt, and black pepper to your Instant Pot. Stir until well combined.
- Stir in the soaked navy beans.
- Lock the lid and cook at high pressure for 35 minutes.
- When the cooking is done, naturally release the pressure for 10 minutes and quick release any remaining pressure. Remove the lid.
- Stir in the cooked bacon and press "saute" function. Simmer the beans, stirring occasionally, until the sauce reaches your desired consistency.

- Serve and enjoy!

Nutrition information per serving:
- Calories: 264
- Fat: 6.1g
- Carbohydrates: 40g
- Dietary Fiber: 9.5g
- Protein: 13.6g

17. Classic Potato Salad

Time: 10 minutes + 1 hour of refrigerating time
Servings: 8
Freestyle SmartPoints: 3
Ingredients:
- 6 medium russet potatoes, peeled and cubed
- 1 ½ cup of water
- 4 large eggs
- ¼ cup of onions, finely chopped
- 1 cup of fat-free mayonnaise
- 2 tablespoons of parsley
- 1 tablespoon of pickle juice
- 1 tablespoon of mustard
- ½ teaspoon of salt
- ½ teaspoon of black pepper

Instructions:
- Place a steamer basket inside your Instant Pot.
- Add the water, potatoes, and eggs.
- Lock the lid and cook at high pressure for 4 minutes.
- When the cooking is done, quick release the pressure and remove the lid.
- Remove the steamer basket from your Instant Pot and place the eggs in an ice bath.
- Allow the potatoes to cool. Peel and dice the cooled eggs.
- In a large bowl, combine the onions, mayonnaise, pickle juice, and mustard.
- Stir in the potatoes and eggs into the potato salad.
- Season with salt and black pepper. Refrigerate for 1 hour before serving.

Nutrition information per serving:
- Calories: 258
- Fat: 12.2g
- Carbohydrates: 32.7g
- Dietary Fiber: 3.9g
- Protein: 5.8g

18. Contest-Winning Chili Con Carne

Time: 20 minutes
Servings: 8
Freestyle SmartPoints: 8
Ingredients:
- 1 pound of ground beef
- 1 (28-ounce) can of whole peeled tomatoes, undrained
- 1 (14-ounce) can of black beans, rinsed and drained
- 1 (14-ounce) can of kidney beans, rinsed and drained
- 3 tablespoons of olive oil
- 1 large onion, finely chopped
- 1 red bell pepper, chopped
- 2 medium jalapenos, chopped
- 2 garlic cloves, minced
- 1 teaspoon of ground cumin
- 1 tablespoon of chili powder
- 1 teaspoon of dried oregano
- 1 ½ teaspoon of salt
- ½ teaspoon of black pepper

Instructions:
- Press "saute" function on your Instant Pot and add the olive oil.
- Once the oil is hot and ready, add the ground beef and cook until brown, breaking it into smaller pieces with a spoon.
- Add the onions, bell pepper, and jalapenos into your Instant Pot and cook for 3 minutes.
- Add the garlic, cumin, chili powder, oregano, salt, and black pepper. Cook for 1 minute, stirring occasionally.
- Add the Worcestershire sauce, tomatoes, water, and beans. Stir until well combined.
- Lock the lid on your Instant Pot and cook at high pressure for 10 minutes.
- When the cooking is done, naturally release the pressure for 10 minutes and quick release any remaining pressure.
- Press "saute" function and cook until the chili has thickened or reached your desired consistency. Serve and enjoy!

Nutrition information per serving:
- Calories: 519
- Fat: 10.3g
- Carbohydrates: 68.6g
- Dietary Fiber: 17g

- Protein: 40.4g

19. Drive-Thru Tacos

Time: 20 minutes
Servings: 4
Freestyle SmartPoints: 6
Ingredients:
- 1 pound of ground beef
- 1 tablespoon of Worcestershire sauce
- 1 tablespoon of olive oil
- 1 cup of beef broth
- 2 teaspoons of all-purpose flour
- 1 tablespoon of chili powder
- ¼ teaspoon of garlic powder
- ¼ teaspoon of onion powder
- ¼ teaspoon of dried minced onions
- 1 ½ teaspoon of ground cumin
- ¼ teaspoon of dried oregano
- ½ teaspoon of paprika
- 1 teaspoon of salt
- ½ teaspoon of black pepper
- A pinch of cayenne pepper
- Taco shells (for serving)

Instructions:
- Press "saute" function on your Instant Pot and add the olive oil.
- Once hot and ready, add the ground beef and cook until brown, stirring occasionally.
- Turn off "saute" function.
- Add the remaining ingredients in your Instant Pot. Stir until well combined.
- Lock the lid and cook at high pressure for 3 minutes.
- When the cooking is done, naturally release the pressure for 10 minutes and quick release any remaining pressure.
- Remove the lid and press "saute" function. Mix and allow to simmer until most of the liquid has reduced.
- Spoon the taco meat onto taco shells.
- Serve and enjoy!

Nutrition information per serving:
- Calories: 259
- Fat: 10.9g
- Carbohydrates: 2g
- Dietary Fiber: 0g
- Protein: 35.7g

20. Fun to Eat Monkey Bread

Time: 25 minutes
Servings: 8
Freestyle SmartPoints: 5
Ingredients:
- 3 ½ cups of all-purpose flour
- ¾ cups of sugar
- ¼-ounces of active dry variety yeast
- 1 teaspoon of salt
- 1 cup of low-fat milk
- ½ cup of unsalted butter softened
- 1 large egg, beaten
- 1 teaspoon of ground cinnamon
- ¼ teaspoon of ground nutmeg
- 1/8 teaspoon of cloves

Instructions:
- In a large bowl, add 1 ½ cup of all-purpose flour, ¼ cup of sugar, yeast, and salt. Mix well.
- Use an electric mixer and gradually beat in the milk and ¼ cup of butter.
- Add the egg and remaining flour and beat for 2 minutes.
- Turn the dough onto a floured counter and knead until smooth and elastic.
- Cover the dough with plastic wrap and allow to rest for 10 minutes.
- In a small bowl, add ¼ cup of melted butter.
- In a second bowl, add ½ cup of sugar, cinnamon, nutmeg, and cloves.
- Divide the dough into 4 quarters.
- Dip each dough quarter into the butter mixture and coat well with the sugar mixture.
- Place the biscuit pieces into a greased mini loaf pan.
- Add 1 cup of water and a trivet to your Instant Pot.
- Place the loaf pan on top of the trivet. Cover with a piece of aluminum foil.
- Lock the lid and cook at high pressure for 21 minutes.
- When the cooking is done, naturally release the pressure for 5 minutes and quick release any remaining pressure.
- Remove the lid and allow the bread to cool Serve and enjoy!

Nutrition information per serving:
- Calories: 398
- Fat: 13.3g

- Carbohydrates: 62.4g
- Dietary Fiber: 1.7g
- Protein: 7.9g

21. Perfect Little Smokies

Time: 10 minutes

Servings: 8

Freestyle SmartPoints: 2

Ingredients:
- 2 (12-ounce) packages of Cocktail Sausages
- 8-ounces of barbecue sauce
- ¼ cup of light brown sugar
- 1 tablespoon of white vinegar
- 1 tablespoon of honey
- 4-ounces of beer

Instructions:
- Add the sausages to your Instant Pot.
- Add the barbecue sauce, brown sugar, white vinegar, honey, and beer to the sausages. Stir until well combined.
- Lock the lid and cook at high pressure for 1 minute.
- When the cooking is done, naturally release the pressure for 1 minute and quick release the remaining pressure.
- Press "Saute" in your Instant Pot. Cook and stir for 5 minutes to thicken the sauce.
- Serve and enjoy!

Nutrition information per serving:
- Calories: 363
- Fat: 24.2g
- Carbohydrates: 17.4g
- Dietary Fiber: 0.2g
- Protein: 16.6g

Desserts Recipes

1. Beautiful Lemon-Blueberry Bundt Cake

Time: 40 minutes

Servings: 8

Freestyle SmartPoints: 7

Ingredients:
- 3 cups of all-purpose flour
- 2 cups of sugar
- 1 teaspoon of baking powder
- ¾ teaspoons of baking soda
- ½ teaspoon of salt
- ½ teaspoon of ground cinnamon
- ¼ teaspoon of ground nutmeg
- 1 cup of low-fat buttermilk
- 3 large eggs, beaten
- ½ cup of coconut oil
- 3 teaspoons of lemon zest, grated
- ½ teaspoon of vanilla extract
- 2 cups of fresh or frozen blueberries

Instructions:
- In a bowl, add the flour, sugar, baking powder, baking soda, salt, cinnamon, and nutmeg. Stir until well combined.
- In a second bowl, add the buttermilk, eggs, coconut oil, lemon zest, and vanilla extract.
- Combine the buttermilk mixture with the flour mixture and stir until well combined. Fold in the blueberries.
- Grease a 6-cup bundt pan with nonstick cooking spray.
- Pour the batter into the bundt cake pan.
- Tightly wrap the bundt cake pan with aluminum foil.
- Add 1 cup of water and a trivet inside your Instant Pot.
- Place the bundt pan inside your Instant Pot.
- Lock the lid and cook at high pressure for 25 minutes.
- When the cooking is done, naturally release the pressure for 10 minutes and quick release any remaining pressure. Carefully remove the lid and remove the pan.
- Allow the cake to cool. Serve and enjoy!

Nutrition information per serving:
- Calories: 538
- Fat: 16.4g
- Carbohydrates: 93.3g
- Dietary Fiber: 2.3g
- Protein: 8.5g

2. Sensational Apples with Oats

Time: 15 minutes

Servings: 4

Freestyle SmartPoints: 2

Ingredients:
- 5 medium-size apples, peeled and chopped
- 2 teaspoons of cinnamon
- ½ teaspoon of nutmeg
- ½ cup of water
- 1 tablespoon of maple syrup
- 4 tablespoons of butter
- ¾ cup of old-fashioned rolled oats
- ¼ cup of flour
- ¼ cup of brown sugar
- ½ teaspoon of salt

Instructions:
- Add the apple chunks inside your Instant Pot.
- In a bowl, add and mix the remaining ingredients and spoon over the apples.
- Close the lid and cook at high pressure for 8 minutes.
- When the cooking is done, naturally release the pressure and remove the lid.
- Serve and enjoy!

Nutrition information per serving:
- Calories: 381
- Fat: 13.1g
- Carbohydrates: 67.1g
- Dietary Fiber: 8.5g
- Protein: 3.7g

3. Best Chocolate Pudding

Time: 30 minutes

Servings: 6

Freestyle SmartPoints: 4

Ingredients:
- 1 ½ cups of whipping cream
- 4-ounces of bittersweet chocolate, chopped
- 4 egg yolks
- 1/3 cup of brown sugar, packed
- 1 tablespoon of unsweetened cocoa powder

- 1 teaspoon of vanilla extract
- ¼ teaspoon of salt
- 1 ½ cup of water

Instructions:

- In a medium saucepan, add the whipping cream and heat over medium heat.
- Remove from the heat and add the chocolate. Stir until the chocolate is melted.
- In a large bowl, add the egg yolks, brown sugar, cocoa powder, vanilla extract, and salt. Mix until well blended.
- Gradually stir in the hot chocolate mixture until well blended together.
- Strain the mixture into a 7-inch soufflé dish or round baking dish that is suitable for your Instant Pot.
- Tightly cover with aluminum foil.
- Add 1 ½ cup of water and a trivet inside your Instant Pot.
- Place the soufflé dish on top of the trivet.
- Close and seal the lid and cook at low pressure at 22 minutes.
- When the cooking is done, naturally release the pressure for 5 minutes and quick release the remaining pressure.
- Remove the lid and carefully remove the soufflé dish from your Instant Pot.
- Refrigerate the soufflé dish for at least 3 hours or if you prefer you can eat it hot or warm. Serve and enjoy!

Nutrition information per serving:

- Calories: 259
- Fat: 18g
- Carbohydrates: 21g
- Dietary Fiber: 0.9g
- Protein: 4.1g

4. Great Lemon Buttermilk Bundt Cake

Time: 35 minutes

Servings: 16

Freestyle SmartPoints: 8

Ingredients:

- 2 ½ cups of all-purpose flour
- 1 teaspoon of baking soda
- 1 teaspoon of baking powder
- 1 teaspoon of salt
- 1 cup of uncooked beets, peeled and finely grated
- 1 cup of low-fat buttermilk
- 8 teaspoons of lemon juice
- 1 tablespoon of lemon zest
- 6 tablespoons of unsalted butter, softened
- 1 ¼ cups of sugar
- 2 large eggs, beaten
- 1 tablespoon of vanilla extract

Glazing ingredients:

- 4-ounces of cream cheese softened
- 1/3 cups of powdered sugar
- 2 tablespoons of low-fat milk
- 1 teaspoon of vanilla extract

Instructions:

- Grease a bundt pan with nonstick cooking spray.
- In a large bowl, add the flour, baking soda, baking powder, and salt.
- In a second bowl, add the beets, buttermilk, lemon juice, and lemon zest. Mix well.
- In a third bowl, add and beat the sugar and butter until fluffy.
- Add the eggs one by one and 1 tablespoon of vanilla extract; beat well.
- Add the beet mixture and flour mixture into the bowl and mix until well combined.
- Spoon the batter into the greased bundt pan and tightly cover with aluminum foil.
- Add 1.5 cups of water and a trivet inside your Instant Pot.
- Lock and close the lid on your Instant Pot. Cook at high pressure for 25 minutes.
- When the cooking is done, quick release the pressure and remove the lid.
- Carefully remove the bundt pan and allow to cool.
- To make the glaze: in a medium bowl, add the cream cheese, powdered sugar, low-fat milk, and 1 teaspoon of vanilla extract. Mix until well combined.
- Drizzle the glaze evenly over the cooled cake. Slice into 16 pieces. Serve!

Nutrition information per serving:

- Calories: 221
- Fat: 7.8g
- Carbohydrates: 34g
- Dietary Fiber: 0.8g
- Protein: 4.2g

5. Secret Chocolate Cupcakes

Time: 40 minutes

Servings: 8

Freestyle SmartPoints: 4

Cupcake Ingredients:
- 1 box of chocolate cake mix
- 1 (15-ounce) can of pumpkin
- ¼ cup of water

Frosting ingredients:
- ¼ cup of peanut butter
- 1 teaspoons of cocoa powder
- 2 tablespoons of maple syrup

Instructions:
- In a large bowl, add and mix all the cupcake ingredients.
- Fill silicone cupcake liners ¾ full. If you don't have silicone cupcake liners, you can use ramekins or heat-safe glass jars. Cover with aluminum foil.
- Add 1 ½ cups of water and a trivet inside your Instant Pot.
- Place the cupcakes on the trivet.
- Close the lid and cook at high pressure for 25 minutes.
- When the cooking is done, naturally release the pressure and remove the lid.
- Carefully remove the cupcakes and allow to cool.
- In a bowl, add and mix all the frosting ingredients until well combined.
- Spoon the frosting on top of the cupcakes.
- Serve and enjoy

Nutrition information per serving:
- Calories: 359
- Fat: 14.5g
- Carbohydrates: 57.2g
- Dietary Fiber: 3.7g
- Protein: 6.5g

6. Satisfying Blueberry Compote

Time: 20 minutes

Servings: 2

Freestyle SmartPoints: 4

Ingredients:
- 3 cups of frozen blueberries
- ¾ cups of sugar
- 2 tablespoons of lemon juice
- 2 tablespoons of cornstarch
- 2 tablespoons of water

Instructions:
- Add the blueberries, sugar, and lemon juice inside your Instant Pot. Stir until well combined.
- Lock the lid and cook at high pressure for 3 minutes.
- When the cooking is done, naturally release the pressure for 10 minutes and quick release any remaining pressure.
- In a small bowl, mix the cornstarch with the water.
- Press saute on your Instant Pot and stir in the cornstarch mixture until thickened.
- Place in a storage container and refrigerate for at least 3 hours.
- Serve and enjoy!

Nutrition information per serving:
- Calories: 440
- Fat: 0.9g
- Carbohydrates: 114.1g
- Dietary Fiber: 5.4g
- Protein: 1.9g

7. Elegant Blackberry Cobbler

Time: 20 minutes

Servings: 6

Freestyle SmartPoints: 6

Ingredients:
- 1 (12-ounce) package of fresh blackberries, washed and dry
- 8-ounces of white cake mix
- ¼ cup of butter
- 1 cup of water

Instructions:
- Grease an oven safe dish that will fit in your Instant Pot with nonstick cooking spray.
- Add the blackberries to the dish.
- In a bowl, using a pastry blender cut the butter into the cake mix until resembles crumbly texture.
- Spread the cake mixture over the blackberries.
- Tightly cover with aluminum foil.
- Add 1 cup of water and a trivet inside your Instant Pot.
- Place the oven safe dish on top.
- Lock the lid of your Instant Pot and cook at high pressure for 10 minutes.

- When the cooking is done, naturally release the pressure for 10 minutes and quick release any remaining pressure.
- Remove the lid and carefully remove the dish from your Instant Pot.
- Allow cooling for 10 minutes.
- Serve and enjoy!

Nutrition information per serving:
- Calories: 253
- Fat: 12.1g
- Carbohydrates: 34.9g
- Dietary Fiber: 3.4g
- Protein: 2.6g

8. Glorious Chocolate Chip Bundt Cake

Time: 40 minutes

Servings: 12

Freestyle SmartPoints: 6

Ingredients:
- 1 (16.5-ounces) of chocolate fudge cake mix
- 2 tablespoons of all-purpose flour
- 1 (3-ounce) package of chocolate dry pudding mix
- 1 cup of buttermilk
- ½ cup of warm water
- ¼ cup of unsweetened applesauce
- 2 tablespoons of coconut oil
- 1 teaspoon of vanilla extract
- 2 large eggs, beaten
- 1 cup of chocolate chips

Topping ingredients:
- 2 tablespoons of powdered sugar

Instructions:
- In a large bowl, add all the cake ingredients except for the chocolate chips and mix until well combined.
- Fold in the chocolate chips.
- Grease a bundt pan with nonstick cooking spray.
- Pour the cake batter into the greased bundt pan.
- Tightly cover the bundt pan with aluminum foil.
- Add 1 ½ cups of water and a trivet inside your Instant Pot.
- Place the bundt pan on top of the trivet and close the lid.
- Cook at high pressure for 25 minutes.
- When the cooking is done, quick release the pressure and remove the lid.
- Carefully remove the cake from your Instant Pot and allow to cool for 10 minutes. Sprinkle powdered sugar over the cake. Serve and enjoy!

Nutrition information per serving:
- Calories: 291
- Fat: 11.6g
- Carbohydrates: 42g
- Dietary Fiber: 1g
- Protein: 4.7g

9. Enticing Pumpkin Chocolate Chip Bundt Cake

Time: 35 minutes

Servings: 8

Freestyle SmartPoints: 8

Ingredients:
- 1 ½ cups of all-purpose flour
- 1 teaspoon of pumpkin pie spice
- 1 teaspoon of ground cinnamon
- 1/4 teaspoon of salt
- ½ teaspoon of baking soda
- ½ teaspoon of baking powder
- ½ cup of butter softened
- 1 cup of sugar
- 2 large eggs, beaten
- 1 cup of pumpkin puree
- ¾ cups of mini-chocolate chips

Instructions:
- In a bowl, add the flour, pumpkin pie spice, cinnamon, salt, baking soda, and baking powder. Mix well.
- In another bowl, beat the butter and sugar until fluffy.
- Mix in the eggs one at a time.
- Add the pumpkin and mix until well combined.
- Add the flour mixture and mix until well combined.
- Fold in the chocolate chips.
- Grease a 6-cup bundt pan with nonstick cooking spray.
- Spoon the batter into the bundt pan. Tightly cover with aluminum foil.
- Add 1 ½ cup of water and a trivet inside your Instant Pot.

- Put the bundt pan on the trivet.
- Close and lock the lid. Cook at high pressure for 25 minutes.
- When the cooking is done, naturally release the pressure for 10 minutes and quick release any remaining pressure.
- Carefully remove the lid and carefully remove the bundt pan.
- Allow cooling for 10 minutes. Serve and enjoy!

Nutrition information per serving:
- Calories: 395
- Fat: 17.8g
- Carbohydrates: 55.4g
- Dietary Fiber: 2.3g
- Protein: 5.7g

10. Delightful Banana Chocolate-Chip Mini Muffins

Time: 10 minutes
Servings: 16
Freestyle SmartPoints: 4
Ingredients:
- 1 cup of vanilla yogurt
- ½ cup of fat-free skim milk
- 1/2 cup of quick oats
- ½ teaspoon of vanilla extract
- 1 large egg, beaten
- 1 large bananas, mashed
- 1 ¼ cup of all-purpose flour
- ¼ cup of brown sugar
- 2 teaspoons of baking powder
- ½ teaspoon of salt
- ½ teaspoon of baking soda
- ½ cup of mini-chocolate chips, divided

Instructions:
- In a bowl, add the milk, vanilla yogurt, vanilla extract, and eggs. Mix until well combined.
- Add the quick oats, bananas, flour, brown sugar, baking powder, salt, and baking soda. Stir until well combined.
- Fold in the chocolate chips.
- Add 1 cup of water and a trivet inside your Instant Pot.
- Using a cookie scoop, fill silicone muffins with the batter.
- Layer the muffin cups inside your Instant Pot. (Note: You may need to cook the muffins in batches if any leftover batter.)
- Cover the muffin cups with aluminum foil to prevent water from resting on top.
- Close and seal your Instant Pot.
- Cook at high pressure for 8 minutes.
- When the cooking is done, naturally release the pressure and remove the lid.
- Check if the muffins are done using a toothpick.
- Remove the muffins and allow to cool. Serve and enjoy!

Nutrition information per serving:
- Calories: 107
- Fat: 2.5g
- Carbohydrates: 17.7g
- Dietary Fiber: 0.9g
- Protein: 3.3g

Chapter 6: 14-Day Healthy Weight Watchers Meal Plan for Beginners

In this chapter, you will find a very effective Weight Watchers Freestyle menu. This menu gives you loads of options to choose on. It can also feed a family of 4. This menu is based on 25 SmartPoints per day but allows you to adjust the meal plan if necessary. Feel free to switch up anything or add more to the menu depending on your preference.

(Note: When locating these recipes, please click on the link or refer to the Table of Contents at the beginning of the book)

Week One
Day One
Meal One: Deluxe Vegan Barbacoa Mushroom Tacos
Meal Two: Spicy Sweet Potato Chili
Meal Three: Grand Leg of Lamb
Day Two
Meal One: Pleasant Fish and Potato Chowder
Meal Two: Fantastic Beef Rice Pilaf
Meal Three: Gorgeous Lemon-Shrimp Risotto with Vegetables and Parmesan
Day Three
Meal One: Hearty Golden Lentil and Spinach Soup
Meal Two: Creamy Macaroni and Cheese
Meal Three: Gratifying Pork Tenderloin with Soy Singer Sauce
Day Four
Meal One: Intriguing Vegan Red Lentil, Sweet Potato, Hemp Burgers
Meal Two: Worldwide Vegetable Soup
Meal Three: Summer Italian Chicken
Day Five
Meal One: Lovely Curry Cauliflower and Broccoli Soup
Meal Two: Charming Chicken Adobo
Meal Three: Decorated Salmon, Broccoli, and Potatoes
Day Six
Meal One: Lip-Smacking Mushroom Stroganoff
Meal Two: Appetizing Tomato Mac and Cheese with Crispy Bacon
Meal Three: Famous Spaghetti
Day Seven
Meal One: Satisfying Vegan Quinoa Burrito Bowls
Meal Two: Signature Curried Chickpea Stuffed Acorn Squash
Meal Three: Rich Honey Teriyaki Chicken
Week Two
Day One
Meal One: Delicious Roasted Onion Garlic Hummus
Meal Two: Pleasant Fish and Potato Chowder
Meal Three: Creamy Tortellini, Spinach, and Chicken Soup
Day Two
Meal One: Famous French Onion Soup
Meal Two: Great Tasting Sweet Potatoes

Meal Three: Tantalizing Beer-And-Mustard Pulled Turkey

Day Three

Meal One: Incredible Wild Mushroom Rice Risotto

Meal Two: Enjoyable Pizza Dip

Meal Three: Marvelous Vegan Black Bean Chili

Day Four

Meal One: Overpowering Wild Rice Soup

Meal Two: Delectable Curry Pumpkin

Meal Three: Louisiana-Style Seafood Chicken, and Sausage Gumbo

Day Five

Meal One: Indian-Inspired Pickled Potatoes

Meal Two: Creamy Tortellini, Spinach, and Chicken Soup

Meal Three: Flavorsome Chunky Beef, Cabbage, and Tomato Soup

Day Six

Meal One: Exquisite Broccoli Cheese Soup

Meal Two: Great Tasting Broccoli and Cheddar Pasta

Meal Three: Out Of This World Balsamic Chicken with Tomatoes and Greens

Day Seven

Meal One: Deluxe Vegan Barbacoa Mushroom Tacos

Meal Two: Mexican-Style Corn on the Cob with Hemp-Lime Sauce

Meal Three: Super Yummy Mediterranean Lamb Roast with Potatoes

Just as a reminder, this is only a sample 2-week meal plan for you to follow to get started with the Weight Watchers program. Feel free to switch up the menu or eat anything with relatively low SmartPoints for that manner.

The Final Words

Thank you very much for downloading and reading this book about the Weight Watchers Program!

After reading this book, you got to know what the Weight Watchers program is, how to get started, how to stick with it, and 120 Weight Watchers Freestyle SmartPoints recipes using your Instant Pot! You also have a 2-week sample meal plan and tips for succeeding in this program. With all that, I am certain you will see positive results following this program.

Thank you, and the best of blessings on your weight loss journey!

Cooking and Culinary Units Conversion Chart

If you can quickly convert measurements of recipes, it will save you a ton of time. The cooking conversion chart below can act as a quick reference list when you follow any of the cookbook's recipes.

Unit:	Equals:	Ounces:	Volume:	Weight:
Pinch	1/16 teaspoon	N/A	N/A	N/A
Dash	1/8 teaspoon	N/A	N/A	N/A
1 teaspoon	N/A	N/A	5 milliliters	N/A
1 tablespoon	3 teaspoons	1/3 ounce	15 milliliters	14.3 grams
1/8 cup	2 tablespoons	1 ounce	30 milliliters	28.3 grams
¼ cup	4 tablespoons	2 ounces	60 milliliters	56.7 grams
½ cup	8 tablespoons	4 ounces	120 milliliters	113.4 grams or ¼ pound
¾ cup	12 tablespoons	6 ounces	180 milliliters	
1 cup	16 tablespoons	8 ounces	240 milliliters	225 grams or ½ pound
1 pint	32 tablespoons or 2 cups	16 ounces	500 milliliters	450 grams or 1 pound
1 quart	4 cups or 2 pints	32 ounces	95 liter	N/A
1 gallon	16 cups or 4 quarts	128 ounces	3.79 liters	N/A

CPSIA information can be obtained
at www.ICGtesting.com
Printed in the USA
LVHW051234130521
687336LV00005B/77

JUN 1 4 2021

9 781801 212045